# The Impact of Tablet PCs and Pen-based Technology on Education

# The Impact of Tablet PCs and Pen-based Technology on Education

## Going Mainstream

## 2010

Edited by
Robert H. Reed and Dave A. Berque

**Purdue University Press**
**West Lafayette, Indiana**

Library of Congress Cataloging-in-Publication Data

The impact of tablet PCs and pen-based technology on education : going mainstream, 2010 / edited by Robert H. Reed and Dave A. Berque.
   p. cm.
   Includes bibliographical references and index.
   ISBN 978-1-55753-574-0
   1. Education--Data processing. 2. Pen-based computers. 3. Education--Effect of technological innovations on. I. Reed, Robert H., 1967- II. Berque, Dave A., 1963-
   LB1028.43.I46 2010
   371.33'4416--dc22
                                             2010040248

# Contents

PART TWO

*Abstracts*

# Preface

## Introduction

This monograph marks the 5<sup>th</sup> Workshop on the Impact of Pen-based Technology on Education (WIPTE). The driving force behind our efforts continues to be our desire to leverage participants' shared interest in educational uses of Tablet PCs and other types of pen-based computing, and to help identify best practices so that all educators can benefit from this technology. The four previous monographs have covered a broad range of subject areas and approaches to using pen-based technology to support teaching and learning. This year's contributions continue to deepen our understanding of how learning environments can be enhanced with pen-based technology, and include several compelling instances that illustrate how technology can help make student learning processes visible to instructors. Every year, the hard work of the educators who contribute time and effort to this book reenergizes the editors. Especially since we recognize that the author's contributions to this work is just one indication of their ongoing commitments to enhance learning.

## Purpose of the Monograph

Collectively, the 2006 [ISBN:1557534349], 2007 [ISBN:1557534616], 2008 [ISBN:1557535313], and 2009 [ISBN: 1557535477] WIPTE Monographs have reported on studies that involved over 8,500 students and more than 110 faculty members from K-12 and higher education; these studies have included disciplines including anatomy, architecture, biomedical engineering, chemistry, computer science, economics, engineering, liberal arts, math, music, and physics. This collection of educators from different areas are using pen-based technology to innovate in ways that make a difference in the teaching and learning ecosystem.

The purpose of this monograph is to share the papers presented at WIPTE 2010, which provide solid evaluation data and discuss issues of broad applicability to pen-based pedagogy. When these papers are considered alongside the works published in previous monographs, evaluations of the pen-based computing experiences of more than 11,000 students are presented. With each additional monograph, we build a larger data set and a larger and more pen-capable community of educators, while also facilitating collaboration between people working in this area.

## Monograph Organization

This monograph is organized in two parts. The first part includes fifteen full-length peer-reviewed papers that report on the application and evaluation of pen-based technology in a wide range of educational settings and subject areas. The second part includes fifteen short abstracts that summarize the shorter papers and posters that rounded out the 2010 WIPTE program.

Below is a summary of quantitative data from each of the papers. The reader will notice a range of papers from K-12 and higher education as well as numerous subject areas. We highly recommend the reader take the time to review each paper in its entirety for all of the quantitative and qualitative data and conclusions presented.

## Conclusions

WIPTE 2010 brought together a group of educators from diverse backgrounds who share a serious commitment to using Tablet PCs and other forms of pen-based technology to support teaching and learning. The sharing of experiences and best practices during the workshop continues to provide the basis for a new community of tablets-in-education researchers, practitioners, and thought leaders. To participate in this community, please visit www.wipte.org.

A special thanks to the WIPTE 2010 organizing committee:
Rob Baker – Cincinnati Country Day School
Dave Berque – DePauw University
Bob Farrow – Fujitsu
Mark Payton – King's Academy (Jordan)
Rob Reed – International Society for Technology in Education
Joe Tront – Virginia Polytechnic Institute
Zvi Ritz – University of Illinois at Urbana-Champaign
Michael Vasey – DyKnow
Tom Walker – Virginia Polytechnic Institute

We also thank the contributing authors, the many volunteer reviewers, and Katherine Purple at Purdue University Press for their cooperation and hard work. With every WIPTE, we are seeing a higher quality of papers, presentations, and innovations; bringing these works to you is truly a shared effort.

We have been fortunate in attracting generous sponsors each year, enabling us to provide a high quality program at a very low cost to the attendees. We would like to thank the WIPTE 2010 corporate sponsors: Hewlett-Packard, DyKnow, Fujitsu, Intel, and Microsoft Research for their financial and logistical support.

And finally, we appreciate your interest in trying to make a difference in education.

Dave Berque and Rob Reed
Editors

**Table 1.** Summary of full-length papers from Part One of this volume.

| First Author | Context K-12 | Context Hi Ed | N | Group Assessed | Course/Field/Discipline |
|---|---|---|---|---|---|
| Bryfczynski | | X | 2000+ | Students | Chemistry |
| Carruthers | | X | 115 | Students | Math |
| Frolik | | X | 38 | Students | Systems Thinking |
| Garrick | | X | 27 | Students | Pneumatics and Hydraulics |
| Graves | | X | 11 | SWLD* students | Multiple Disciplines |
| Hamilton | X | | 21 | Instructors | Math |
| Hatfield | | X | 100 | Students | Computer Science |
| Hayden | | X | 3 | Low Vision Students | Multiple Disciplines |
| Hieb | | X | 27 | Students | Linear Algebra |
| Hrepic | | X | 37 | Students | Physics |
| Koile | X | X | 400 | Students | Math |
| Logan | | X | 99 | Students | Biology, History, and Philosophy |
| Porter | | X | 429 | Students | Statistics |
| Romney | | X | 50 | Students | Math |
| Wangberg | | X | 43 | Students | Calculus |

* students with learning disabilities

# Contributor and Editor Information

**Beya Adamu** is an undergraduate student majoring in computer science at Winona State University.

E-mail: adamu.beya@gmail.com

**Catherine Amelink** serves as the Assessment Coordinator for the Division of Student Affairs at Virginia Polytechnic and State University. She works with program review activities, data analysis, and assessment of learning outcomes.

E-mail: amelink@vt.edu

**Eric Anderson** is a graduate student in computer science at Clemson University. He has been funded by the National Science Foundation to research and develop many different aspects of MessageGrid.

E-mail: enanders@clemson.edu

**Nicole Anderson** is an assistant professor teaching undergraduate courses in computer science at Winona State University. Her research interests include utilizing technological tools that also build new learning communities.

E-mail: nanderson@winona.edu

**Norhayati Baharun** is a doctoral student senior lecturer at the University of Wollongong. She has taught in universities in Malaysia and Australia. Her research is on improving mathematics and statistics outcomes through the application and improvement of learning designs.

E-mail: nbb470@uow.edu.au

**Nathan Bailey**, the architect of Monash's staff and student my.monash portal, currently oversees a range of educational projects as Associate Director of the eEducation Centre at Monash University.

E-mail: nathan.bailey@monash.edu

**Robert Baker** is the Director of Technology at the Cincinnati Country Day School. He is dedicated to evangelizing about the power of Tablet PCs. He hosts three Tablet PC conferences that allow Cincinnati Country Day School to collaborate with educators from around the world.

E-mail: baker@countryday.net

**José-V. Benlloch-Dualde** teaches undergraduate computer science courses related to computer technology and multimedia systems at Universidad Politécnica de Valencia. His research interests relate to technology-enhanced learning and pen-based technologies.

E-mail: jbenlloc@disca.upv.es

**Dave A. Berque** teaches a wide range of undergraduate computer science courses at DePauw University. His research interests relate to human-computer interaction, instructional technology, and pen-based computing.

E-mail: dberque@depauw.edu

**Kristin Bertram** is an undergraduate student majoring in mathematics and mathematics education at Winona State University.

E-mail: kmbertra9923@winona.edu

**John A. Black Jr.** is a research scientist at CUbiC, Arizona State University. He researches the abilities and limitations of human vision, with the aim of using technology to enhance visual perception and cognition.

E-mail: john.black@asu.edu

**Terri L. Bonebright** teaches undergraduate psychology courses, with a special emphasis on research methodology, at DePauw University. Her research interests relate to human auditory perception and human-computer interaction.

E-mail: tbone@depauw.edu

**Craig Leonard Brians** is an associate professor and the Associate Department Chair at Virginia Polytechnic and State University. His research analyzes information-seeking and political communication, and his teaching reflects his desire to build students' information fluency skills across the curriculum.

E-mail: cbrians@vt.edu

**Samuel P. Bryfczynski** is a PhD student in computer science at Clemson University and has been developing pedagogical tools for Tablet PCs for five years. He is the main developer of the OrganicPad and GraphPad software..

E-mail: sbryfcz@clemson.edu

**Salvador Buccella** is the Coordinator of University Medical Service at the University of Carabobo.

E-mail: smbuccella@uc.edu.ve

**Félix Buendía** teaches and supervises academic projects related to Web environments at Universidad Politécnica de Valencia. His research interests are Web applications, e-learning, and other related topics.

E-mail: fbuendia@disca.upv.es

**Juan-Carlos Cano** is associate professor of computer architecture and technology at Universidad Politécnica de Valencia and has taught computer engineering since 1995. His current research interests include mobile ad hoc networks, pervasive computing, and pen-based technologies.

E-mail: jucano@disca.upv.es

**Carol Carruthers** is a professor and coordinator teaching mathematics at Seneca College of Applied Arts and Technology. She focuses on bridging alternatives for students entering college programs. Her research reflects her passion for innovative mathematics teaching and learning.

E-mail: carol.carruthers@senecac.on.ca

**Glen P. Ciborowski** teaches undergraduate computer science courses at Bluefield State College. His research interests include information systems, interaction design, project management, and systems analysis.

E-mail: gciborowski@cartinc.com

**Melanie M. Cooper** is the Alumni Distinguished Professor of chemistry and Interim Department Chair at Clemson University. She researches the area of chemistry education and includes assessment and improvement of problem solving, conceptual understanding, and the development of research-validated curriculum materials.

E-mail: cmelani@clemson.edu

**Brian Fisher** teaches the full spectrum of courses in Pepperdine University's mathematics program and conducts research on student conceptions of multivariate limits.

E-mail: brian.fisher@pepperdine.edu

**Paul Flikkema** is a professor of electrical engineering at Northern Arizona University. His interests include wireless communication and networking, sensor networks, statistical inference, complex engineered systems, and pedagogy and technology that improve STEM education.

E-mail: paul.flikkema@nau.edu

**Edward A. Fox** is a professor in the Department of Computer Science at Virginia Polytechnic and State University. He is a member of the CRA Board, executive director of NDLTD (www.ndltd.org), and actively involved in teaching/research/service related to digital libraries, information retrieval, multimedia, and computing education.

E-mail: fox@vt.edu

**Katharina Franke** is a research coordinator who manages the research program at the eEducation Centre at Monash University, involving a range of education, technology, and learning space projects. She occasionally teaches in sociolinguistics.

E-mail: katharina.franke@monash.edu

**Jeff Frolik** is an associate professor of engineering at University of Vermont. He conducts research and teaches undergraduate and graduate courses in sensor networks and wireless communications.

E-mail: jfrolik@uvm.edu

**Robert D. Garrick** is an associate professor of manufacturing and mechanical engineering technology at Rochester Institute of Technology. His primary research interests are in the domain of product realization and energy efficient buildings.

E-mail: rdgmet@rit.edu

**Laura Graves** is an associate professor of early childhood education at Tennessee Technological University. She teaches early childhood, early childhood SPED, and special education courses. Her research interests revolve around learning disabilities at the post-secondary level.

E-mail: lgraves@tntech.edu

**Nathaniel P. Grove** is an assistant professor of chemistry at University of North Carolina Wilmington. He is broadly interested in researching the factors that influence meaningful learning in chemistry.

E-mail: groven@uncw.edu

**Carol Haden** is Senior Evaluation Consultant at Magnolia Consulting, LLC. She specializes in the evaluation of K-20 science education programs.

E-mail: carol@magnoliaconsulting.org

**Chris Hagan**, architect of Monash MeTL, designs and builds cloud-focused applications in highly functional languages.

E-mail: chris.hagan@monash.edu

**David Hagan** is a system administrator and developer at Monash University. He works to support instructors using technology to enhance their teaching by collaborating with students.

E-mail: david.hagan@monash.edu

**Eric Hallerman** is a professor and the Head of the Department of Fisheries and Wildlife Sciences at Virginia Polytechnic and State University. He participates in development and evaluation of tools for species identification and information retrieval.

E-mail: ehallerm@vt.edu

**Eric Hamilton** is a professor and the Associate Dean with joint appointment in mathematics at Pepperdine University. He conducts research in pen-based computing, avatars in learning, and computer-supported collaboration. He has organized an international symposia series on future learning environments.

E-mail: eric.hamilton@pepperdine.edu

**Nancy Harding** is an associate professor of education at Pepperdine University, and she has led Pepperdine University's student teaching program. She is project director for the IES pen-based computing research supported by IES.

E-mail: nancy.harding@pepperdine.edu

**Jared J. Hatfield** is a graduate student in computer engineering and computer science at the University of Louisville specializing in software development for pen- and touch-based interfaces.

E-mail: jjhatf02@louisville.edu

**David S. Hayden** is a graduate research assistant at CUbiC, Arizona State University. He is a National Science Foundation Fellow with research interests in machine learning, computer vision, and assistive technologies.

E-mail: dshayden@asu.edu

**Chelsea Aleena Hickey** is a fourth year University Honors student at Virginia Polytechnic and State University majoring political science and statistics.

E-mail: Hickeyc@vt.edu

**Jeffrey L Hieb** is an assistant professor in the Department of Engineering Fundamentals at the University of Louisville. He teaches undergraduate engineering mathematics courses, and his research interests include cyber security for process control systems, critical thinking education, and pen-based education for engineers.

E-mail: jeff.hieb@louisville.edu

**Zdeslav Hrepic** is assistant professor at Columbus State University. He teaches undergraduate physics and science methods courses, and his research interests include educational technology, cognitive issues in learning, student understanding of traditional lecture, among others.

E-mail: zdeslav_hrepic@colstate.edu

**Kevin Iga** teaches the full spectrum of courses in Pepperdine University's mathematics program and conducts research in differential geometry, manifolds, and supersymmetry.

E-mail: kevin.iga@pepperdine.edu

**Kimberle Koile** is a research scientist at Massachusetts Institute of Technology, Center for Educational Computing Initiatives (MIT CECI), focusing on using Tablet PCs to increase interaction and learning in K-12 and undergraduate settings.

E-mail: kkoile@mit.edu

**Marybeth Koon** is the Instructional Technologist at Rochester Institute of Technology Wallace Center's Teaching, Learning, and Scholarship Services. She works closely with the Academic Technology team to support the TLT Studio, an incubator space for faculty to explore new teaching strategies through the implementation of instructional technology.

E-mail: mjmetc@rit.edu

**Shreya Kothaneth** is a doctoral candidate studying industrial and systems engineering at Virginia Polytechnic and State University. Her research interests include technology acceptance, usability, and creativity.

E-mail: skoth26@vt.edu

**Nadia P. Kozievitch** is a PhD student at the University of Campinas. Her interests include digital libraries and complex objects, applying them in different domains, like GIS, content-based image retrieval (CBIR), and pen-based education.

E-mail: nadiapk@ic.unicamp.br

**Lenin Lemus Zúñiga** teaches undergraduate computer science courses related to computer architecture and local area networks at Universidad Politécnica de Valencia. His research interests relate to Web technologies and e-learning.

E-mail: lemus@disca.upv.es

**Murray Logan** is a research officer at Monash University. He has taught a range of biology subjects and has a passionate interest in the pedagogy of educational technologies and collaborative software.

E-mail: murray.logan@monash.edu

**Chris Malone** is an associate professor and Director of the Winona State University Statistical Consulting Center. He teaches a wide range of undergraduate statistics courses and is interested in the way Tablet PC technology can help create an interactive statistics classroom.

E-mail: cmalone@winona.edu

**Gregory K. Martin** holds a PhD in Shakespeare Studies and is currently responsible for the curriculum review and professional/pedagogical development programs at Cincinnati Country Day School.

E-mail: marting@countryday.net

**Uma Murthy** is a PhD candidate in the Department of Computer Science at Virginia Polytechnic and State University. Her research interests include digital libraries, annotations, information retrieval, personal information management, and natural language processing.

E-mail: umurthy@vt.edu

**Bruce V. Mutter** teaches undergraduate architectural engineering courses at Bluefield State College. His applied research and technology transfer interests include building control systems, project management, and engineering economics.

E-mail: bmutter@bluefieldstate.edu

**Roy P. Pargas** is an associate professor of computer science at Clemson University. He develops Tablet PC-based software for STEM disciplines (chemistry, mathematics, engineering, and computer science).

E-mail: pargas@cs.clemson.edu

**Stacey Plant** is an instructional media specialist at Tennessee Technological University. She takes leading and assisting roles in Tennessee Technological University projects that weave together technology, instruction, and learning. Her interests relate to Web accessible communities.

E-mail: splant@tntech.edu

**Anne Porter** is a lecturer in statistics at the University of Wollongong. She works to improve statistics education, exploring the different pedagogical approaches, assessment techniques, new technologies, learning support, and good learning design.

E-mail: alp@uow.edu.au

**Marilyn Reba** is senior lecturer in the Department of Mathematical Sciences at Clemson University. She has been the principal investigator on several technology grants (e.g., National Science Foundation, Hewlett-Packard).

E-mail: mreba@clemson.edu

**David Reider**, of Education Design, INC, provides educational consulting services to researchers, K-12 schools, post-secondary and adult education institutions, arts organizations, and technology design firms.

E-mail: david@educationdesign.biz

**Kevin J. Reins** teaches graduate and undergraduate courses in mathematics education at The University of South Dakota. His research foci include lesson study with prospective mathematics teachers and collaborative-interactive digital inking practices.

E-mail: Kevin.Reins@usd.edu

**Carla A. Romney** teaches undergraduate mathematics classes at Boston University. Her research focuses on increasing the number of students who successfully complete science or engineering degrees.

E-mail: romney@bu.edu

**Kevin Rokuskie** is the Senior Information Services Consultant at the Cary Academy, grades sixth through eighth. He has worked in the computer field for seventeen years.

E-mail: Kevin_Rokuskie@caryacademy.org

**Andee Rubin** is a senior scientist at TERC. She specializes in research and development in mathematics and mathematical reasoning, technology, and online learning.

E-mail: andee_rubin@terc.edu

**Rowland Saer Hurtado** is the Coordinator of Center for Information and Communication Technologies and Assisted Education (CETICEA) in the Health Science Faculty at the University of Carabobo.

E-mail: rsaer@uc.edu.ve

**Glenda Scales** serves as both Associate Dean for International Programs and Information Technology and Director of the Commonwealth Graduate Engineering Program (CGEP) at Virginia Polytechnic and State University.

E-mail: gscales@vt.edu

**Kimberly Shaw** is an associate professor at Columbus State University. She teaches physics and physical science courses, and her research interest is physics education research, particularly attitudinal and affective factors and classroom environmental factors impacting student learning, and assessment of that learning.

E-mail: shaw_kimberly@colstate.edu

**Carol L. Smith** is Chief Information Officer at DePauw University. She leads programs that empower faculty members and students to leverage technology to support innovative pedagogies that foster effective teaching and learning.

E-mail: clsmith@depauw.edu

**Gino Sorcinelli** teaches courses on organizational effectiveness at the University of Massachusetts Amherst. Prior to this role, he spent six years as human resource director for a corporate data center.

E-mail: gino@som.umass.edu

**Yasmin Tang** is the Coordinator of Special Analysis Center at the University of Carabobo.

E-mail: yatang@uc.edu.ve

**Ricardo Torres** is a professor in the Institute of Computing at the University of Campinas. His research interests include image analysis, content-based image retrieval (CBIR), databases, digital libraries, and geographic information systems.

E-mail: rtorres@ic.unicamp.br

**Katherine Uber** is an undergraduate student majoring in computer science and mathematics at Winona State University.

E-mail: kuber5876@winona.edu

**Sonia M. Underwood** is a PhD student in chemical education at Clemson University. She is broadly interested in the use of technology in exploring issues surrounding the development of representational competence in chemistry.

E-mail: sunderw@ clemson.edu

**Aaron Wangberg** is an assistant professor teaching undergraduate mathematics courses at Winona State University. His interests include exploring how Tablet PC technology can change the way students are allowed to work with online technology.

E-mail: awangberg@winona.edu

**Tom Weller** is a professor of electrical engineering at University of South Florida. He teaches courses in the areas of electromagnetics, RF/microwave circuits, and antennas. His research is in the areas of sensors and microwave circuit design.

E-mail: weller@usf.edu

**Calvin Williams** is the Director of the Center of Excellence in Mathematics and Science Education and is also associate professor of mathematical sciences in the Department of Mathematical Sciences at Clemson University.

E-mail: calvinw@clemson.edu

**Liqing Zhou** is a graduate assistant researcher in the new Product Innovation Program at Arizona State University. Her research interests relate to user-centered design, accessibility design, and universal design.

E-mail: lzhou29@asu.edu

**Editors**

**Dave A. Berque** is professor and chair of computer science at DePauw University. He has published more than twenty-five refereed papers and book chapters and has received several grants from the National Science Foundation. Berque's pen-based computing projects have been discussed in a variety of venues including CNN, *The New York Times*, and *The Chronicle of Higher Education*.

**Robert H. Reed** is a consultant for the International Society for Technology in Education (ISTE). He has fourteen years of experience in the fields of engineering and technology. Prior to working for ISTE, Reed worked in University Relations for Hewlett-Packard and Microsoft Research. Reed has also worked for Deloitte Consulting and taught technology to undergraduates at Indiana University.

# PART ONE

# OrganicPad as a Research Tool: Investigating the Development of Representational Competence in Chemistry

*Samuel P. Bryfczynski, Sonia M. Underwood,*
*Nathaniel P. Grove, Roy P. Pargas,*
*and Melanie M. Cooper*

*Clemson University*

## 1. Abstract

This paper describes several new features of OrganicPad—a Tablet PC molecular structure drawing application—which expand its functionality as a research tool. These main features include: (1) the improved replay of students' work; (2) the creation of Markov chains; and (3) the ability to automatically tag students' work and generate charts of data. OrganicPad now assists teachers in replaying their students' construction of assigned structures, and using a collection of replays, generates Markov chains to help expose commonly utilized problem solving pathways. OrganicPad's automatic tagging is based on predefined substructures, user-created substructures, or a series of rules based upon real-world student data. With the addition of these new features, OrganicPad is now a more useful structural research tool.

## 2. Problem Statement and Context

Students in introductory chemistry courses have many topics to learn. One of the more important is the construction of Lewis structures, two-dimensional visual representations of molecules. Superficially, Lewis structures depict atoms, bonds, and electrons; however, they also convey much more meaningful information about the molecule's chemical and physical properties such as polarity, boiling point, and melting point. A number of studies have documented the struggles that students face in learning how to construct Lewis structures [see reference 1 for a complete list], which we conjecture ultimately stem from the instructional modalities typically utilized to teach students how to construct Lewis structures—primarily using a series of arcane and esoteric rules. Furthermore, students must also learn to grapple with an exceptionally large number of exceptions to the rules. Due to these structures being hand drawn, and that the average chemistry class size at the university level can be quite large, providing immediate feedback and grading of Lewis structures can often be time-consuming.

We believe that technology can help to address many of the limitations identified above and fill a critical formative assessment gap. We also believe, however, that any system must be firmly based upon robust research that takes into account the difficulties that students face while constructing structural representations. Despite the fact that the construction of valid Lewis structures has been a topic of interest for nearly four decades, little actual research has been conducted in this area. The research tools that have been incorporated into OrganicPad will provide opportunities to address this oversight, supplying researchers with better tools to extract and analyze data, and therefore, discover insights into students' cognitive processes and the difficulties they encounter when attempting to construct Lewis structures that would not be available otherwise.

OrganicPad is an attempt to understand how students better utilize chemical structures. OrganicPad was created to allow users to draw Lewis structures without restrictions of atom arrangement or placement and to eliminate interface issues by using a stylus and Tablet PC [2]. OrganicPad works by converting students' handwriting into an interactive structural representation. Its interface is ideal for students, instructors, and researchers as it ensures that students are focusing their attention on the problem instead of the interface. Because of this, we believe OrganicPad provides a compelling research tool to accurately record student work in an interactive form.

This paper describes several new features of OrganicPad and how they are being used by researchers to investigate how students construct Lewis structures. Section 3 describes the features that were added to OrganicPad: submission replay, Markov chain generation, and automatic tagging. Section 4 describes how researchers are utilizing the newly implemented features to conduct research. Section 5 concludes with a brief discussion of our future plans for OrganicPad.

## 3. OrganicPad Improvements

### 3.1 Replay

As previously published, OrganicPad has the ability to replay student work [2]. We have improved this replay system to be more efficient than our previous implementation, which simply made copies of the student work after each step. OrganicPad now records all of the user's submitted work as a list of InkReplayStep objects. Each InkReplayStep object has four variables associated with it: Mode, Ink, Recognition Result, and Graph Difference. The Mode variable records the current mode of the application such as draw, erase, annotate, or select. The Ink variable records the serialized ink strokes written on the screen, while the Recognition Result records the result when OrganicPad uses handwriting recognition to convert the strokes to a text string. Finally, the Graph Difference records the difference between the previous Lewis structure drawn and the current Lewis structure. These four variables allow for OrganicPad to replay the process each student takes when constructing their structures. The Ink strokes are displayed to show the raw input the student made along with the mode that the student was in when drawing. The Recognition Result and Graph Difference allow for an exact recording of the student work to be made without having to copy the entire graph structure for each step as was previously implemented. This allows instructors to not only view the final submission, but the entire process as well in an efficient manner. By pinpointing the position in the replay where students make mistakes, researchers can better identify the errors a student or class are making, which can ultimately lead to insights into the students' cognitive processes.

### 3.2 Markov Chains

In the previous section, we described how OrganicPad can replay student work. While replaying student submissions can uncover information about how students think, manual analysis of individual Lewis structures is time-consuming, and looking at replays can take significantly longer. Therefore, Markov chains were added to allow researchers to view a graphical representation of the results from an entire class of student replays.

The Markov chain construction follows a straightforward algorithm [3]. Pseudo code for the algorithm is shown in Figure 1. The algorithm iterates over a set of replay data from different submissions. For each submission, our algorithm iterates over each step in the replay of that submission. The algorithm then reconstructs the Lewis structure graph for each step using the same approach described in the replay section (3.1). With lists of these graphs, our algorithm first determines (using graph isomorphism [4]) if the current step's graph is already contained in the Markov chain. If a match is found, then a counter on that Markov chain node is incremented. The system then determines if an edge exists in the Markov chain between the previous step and the current step in the replay. If one exists, then the edge's counter is incremented; otherwise, a new edge is created between the previous node and the current node. Finally, if the current step's graph cannot be matched with any node in the Markov chain, a new node is placed in the Markov chain and a new edge between the previous node and the new one is created. This process continues until all of the replay steps from all submissions have been processed. At this point, the system generates the probabilities of movement along paths by dividing the edge's counter value by the starting nodes in-degree. The system uses a graph layout algorithm to layout the Markov chain and presents the final product to the researcher as shown in Figure 2. Each node in the Markov chain represents a unique structure drawn by one or more students while the edges between them represent the probability of a student moving from one structure to the next.

**Figure 1.** Pseudo Code for Markov Chain Construction.

```
foreach Submission in SubmissionList
{
    foreach ReplayStep in Submission
    {
    structureIndex=MarkovChain.Find(ReplayStep.Graph)
    if structureIndex>-1 //found the structure
        {
        MarkovChain.IncrementNode(structureIndex)
        structureIndex=FindEdge(PreviousStep.Graph,ReplayStep.Graph)
        if(edgeIndex>-1)//found a pre-existing edge
            MarkovChain.IncrementEdge(edgeIndex)
        else
            MarkovChain.AddEdge(PreviousStep.Graph,replayStep.Graph)
        }
    else
        {
        MarkovChain.AddNode(Replaystep.Graph)
        MarkovChain.AddEdge(PreviousStep.Graph,replayStep.Graph)
        }
    }
}
```

For simple structures with low node and edge counts (six or fewer nodes), this system works well, and the Markov chain is fairly straightforward as there are a limited number of possible ways that a student can construct their final structures. However, the possible structures a user can draw and the numerous order of the drawings grows exponentially once the structure complexity and number of submissions increases. This can lead to Markov chains with many branching paths and extra "noise," making the subsequent interpretation difficult.

We have implemented several improvements to our system to enhance readability of the Markov chains. Our first solution is to make the Markov chain editable, that is, users can add, delete, or edit the nodes and edges in the Markov chain to either combine paths or to delete them entirely. This automatically updates both the counters on the edges and nodes and the probability on the edges. In addition, a multipurpose slider was incorporated that removes parts of the Markov chain that do not exceed a certain frequency. The slider may be used as a threshold measure where all nodes and edges with counts below the threshold are removed from the display, or alternately, the slider may be used as an opacity measure to dim the nodes and edges with lower weights. Finally, the slider may be used as a thickness measure where higher weighted nodes and edges have bolder lines than lower weighted ones. Using this slider and options, researchers can customize and adjust the results of the Markov chain to display the information in the manner they believe will be most useful in conveying research results.

### 3.3 Automatic Tagging

OrganicPad has the ability to perform automatic grading and tagging of students' work. OrganicPad uses graph isomorphism algorithms to match student work with a solution set. This can generate a simple grade book that may be exported in a variety of formats. OrganicPad can take this common feature even further with its subgraph algorithm, which attempts to map a small graph into a larger one [4]. With subgraph isomorphism, OrganicPad can use either predefined graphs or custom drawn ones and generate frequency counts on submissions, which can include commonly made errors. For example, OrganicPad can generate frequency counts for common errors such as too many bonds to carbon. This is accomplished using a subgraph, which has a carbon with more than four bonds on them. By combining the grade book with automatic tagging, researchers can quickly identify both the students with incorrect submissions and elicit the reasons for those incorrect submission. Further, the automatic tagging system will tag submissions based on the differences between the submission and the correct answer. The tags were created by several researchers based upon the major difficulties students encounter in constructing valid Lewis structures. The process begins when the researcher selects a group of students to analyze. Next, OrganicPad presents the researcher with a list of unique Lewis structures from the submissions along with the frequency count associated with each. The researcher then selects the correct submissions for OrganicPad to use as an answer key, and using graph isomorphism, it attempts to match each submission with the answer key. In the event that no match is found, OrganicPad will take the best match and compare it to the researcher-created error tags. If OrganicPad cannot accurately evaluate the structure, the researcher will be prompted to manually tag the submission. Finally, OrganicPad presents the results to the researcher. All of these results may be export to Excel for further processing and statistics.

**Figure 2.** Example of a Markov chain constructed from replay data. Nodes represent unique graph structures drawn by students. Edges represent the probability of movement from one structure to another.

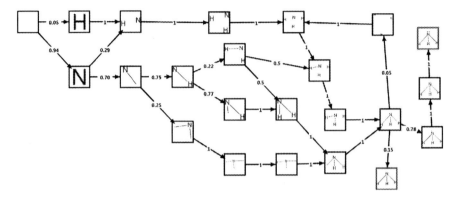

## 4. Evaluation

The features of OrganicPad that are mentioned in this paper (replay, Markov chains, and automatic tagging) are vital for researchers because they allow not only for the understanding of the students' final structures, but more importantly, how they constructed those structures. Altogether, over thirty thousand submissions have been collected from approximately two thousand general and organic chemistry students during a three year period. Currently at Clemson University, there are several streams of research that are utilizing OrganicPad's new features in better understanding how chemistry students develop representational competence. What follows are two specific examples of this use:

1. *How do organic chemistry students' use of the curved-arrow notation to depict electron flow during chemical reactions change over time?* Organic-Pad's replay feature has been used to create Markov models that depict common problem solving pathways that organic chemistry students use when asked to create mechanisms. This information will be used as a guide in helping researchers develop more meaningful instructional approaches.

2. *How do students develop representational competence in creating and utilizing Lewis structures?* All of the above-described features are being used to understand how students construct Lewis structures and to determine the types of problems that students have in doing so.

## 5. Future Work

Our future plans for OrganicPad involves improvements to the Markov chain system. The possible pathways students may take in creating their final structures can grow exponentially even for fairly simple structures. This can result in Markov chains that are cluttered with extra nodes and edges that a researcher likely will find distracting. One possible solution for this problem may involve combining similar paths into one representative path. Our goal is for OrganicPad to present a list of unique pathways that students have created in obtaining their final structures and to then allow the researcher to mark the major sequences with tags. The system will then utilize those tags to cluster sequences and generate a new Markov chain based on the clustered sequences. We plan on accomplishing this process by using sequence clustering algorithms and dynamic programming [3]. In general, sequence clustering algorithms attempt to group sequences that are somehow related [5] and are typically used to cluster protein sequences for bioinformatics. Most of these algorithms use single-linkage clustering to determine similarities between sequences through the use of calculating the nearest neighbor of a part of a sequence and calculating some distance function. By distilling the student-created pathways to a core set of sequences, the Markov chain will be reduced to the main paths that students have taken and thus represent the major cognitive processes that students have utilized.

## 6. Acknowledgments

We gratefully acknowledge support in the form of a 2005 Tablet PC and Computing Curriculum Grant from Microsoft Corporation (Jane Prey, Program Manager), a 2007 Technology for Teaching Leadership Grant from Hewlett-Packard (Jim Vanides, Program Manager), a 2008 NSF ALT Award No. DRL-0735655, and a 2009 Dreyfus Foundation Special Grant Program in the Chemical Sciences.

## References

[1] Cooper, M. M., Grove, N., Underwood, S. M., and Klymkowsky, M. K. Lost in Lewis Structures: An Investigation of Student Difficulties in Developing Representational Competence. *J. Chem. Educ.* DOI: 10.1021/ed900004y.

[2] Cooper, M., Grove, N., Pargas, R., Bryfczynski, S., and Gatlin, T. OrganicPad: An Interactive Freehand Drawing Application for Drawing Lewis Structures and the Development of Skills in Organic Chemistry. *Chem. Educ. Res. Pract.*, 10, 4 (Aug. 2009), 296-301.

[3] Grinstead, M. and Snell, J. Introduction to Probability (2nd Ed). American Mathematical Society, 2006. This work is freely redistributable under the terms of the GNU Free Documentation License.

[4] Toran, J. On the Hardness of Graph Isomorphism, *SIAM J. Comput.*, 33, 5 (2000), 1093-1108.

[5] Kim, S., and Lee, J. BAG: A Graph Theoretic Sequence Clustering Algorithm. *Int. J. of Data Mining and Bioinformatics 1*, 2 (2006), 178-200.

# Engagement and Retention of Marginalized College Students Using Hewlett-Packard Tablet PCs and DyKnow Software

*Carol Carruthers*

*Seneca College of Applied Arts and Technology*

## 1. Abstract

Students in college bridging programs may benefit from having subjects like math and science presented to them using a more innovative teaching style. The use of pen-based Tablet PC technology and interactive software provides the enrichment required to engage and enhance the performance of marginalized students. Data collection of attendance and grades provides insight as to whether or not the use of this technology impacts student learning. Response to surveying gives greater understanding of thinking, and provides the opportunity for students to reflect on this teaching style. Project goals include observation of increasing student engagement, enhancing student learning and concept application, and demonstration of this teaching strategy to other educators. Early indications show that this student-centered, interactive Tablet PC environment results in increased retention and success of students. More testing is required to determine statistical significance. The necessary adaptation in teaching philosophy to ensure students receive the full advantage of this course delivery is also discussed.

## 2. Problem Statement and Context

In the fall of 2008, we developed a bridging program, the Applied Science and Technology (AST) Certificate, to provide a pathway for students whose previous math and science credentials do not meet diploma entry standards. Students who have been absent from formal education, have weak language skills, or lack the self-assurance required to be successful may be similarly marginalized. AST students enroll in a two-semester program designed to strengthen their skills and confidence in mathematics, science, communication, critical thinking, and problem solving. Graduates are guaranteed admission into two-year programs leading to a diploma in applied science, technology, or computer studies.

To assist AST students, a dynamic class environment that resonates with individual learning styles is envisioned for the teaching of math and science. With the receipt of a 2008 Hewlett-Packard Higher Education Technology for Teaching Grant and the purchase of DyKnow software, a collaborative, innovative, and interactive approach to teaching and learning continues to be explored and developed.

Our goals for this project fall under three main categories: increasing student engagement, enhancing student learning and ability to apply concepts, and demonstration of this teaching approach throughout the college/math/technology/outreach communities. This report will focus on the methodologies and results from the investigation of math only, although a similar case can be made for science groups.

## 3. Solution Employed

We offer the AST program at two campuses separated by seventeen kilometers (eleven miles)—one is hosted by an applied science school and the other by an engineering technology school. Students choose their campus depending on geographic proximity, travel preference, or anticipated program destination (electronics, built environment, advanced technology, fire protection, biochemistry, and information arts and technology). One campus is designated as the experimental group, where both teachers and students use stylus-based Tablet PCs, interactive software, and Internet access in their classroom. The AST classes at the other campus are designated as the control group; teachers have a laptop and electronic podium available and students spend up to 40 percent of their class time in a computer lab. Depending on which instructor teaches the control group, lecture notes are projected onto a screen that students copy and solve on paper. Teachers in our control groups make use of the computer labs to have students work with math applets, graphing software, and the online textbook resources. One teacher developed extra practice sheets, giving students time to work in groups to develop mini presentations. Students present at the board, which the instructor said "gave me the opportunity to let them work on . . . their assignments in class . . . it was more like a tutorial session." Students in both experimental and control groups take common tests and a final exam. Over the course of our two-year study, teachers varied depending on faculty allocation requirements: math for the experimental group is taught by three different teachers and the control group by four. Only one AST group is taught at each campus per semester, with average class size ranging from fifteen to twenty students. Data is a compilation of four cohort intakes of two semesters each, spanning the six semesters of the study.

In our experimental mathematics group, Tablet PCs and DyKnow software are used for more than 90 percent of the teaching hours. Teachers prepare Word document notes with content that conveys information or stimulates independent problem solving and virtually print them into the software (called panels), which students log onto. The instructor's panels are projected both on a classroom screen and directly onto each student's Tablet PC. Teachers and students consistently use the stylus to ink in solutions to math problems and enhance their work using multiple colors, highlighters, free hand diagrams, and flow charts. The teachers insert panels as necessary to stimulate collaboration—often ten to fifteen per lecture depending on the topic. Students work at their own pace independently, or can be placed into online groups so that members can view each other's screens and communicate using the chat function. The "share control" feature is employed often during each class, allowing students to become the "temporary instructor" by having their answers to a problem projected onto their classmates' screens. One technique that works well in my math classes is to prepare skill development questions in duplicate and designate the location of independent versus group work. Once all students complete their attempt, screen control is shared with all, and random students provide their solution in a parallel location (designated as shared work). As more than 75 percent of students willingly participate in this activity, group solutions are anonymous, unless individuals choose to self-identify. Each student can then compare their independent answer to one supplied by their peers for class discussion. Using this technique, students self-correct their own work and gain insight into where personal habitual errors occur. An additional benefit of using this methodology is that students have access to multiple peer solutions, rather than only that of the instructor, thereby allowing them to model the processing that most closely resonates with their own learning style. Once students are familiar with the "polling" and "send panel" features of the software, they will often monitor their understanding and send indication of their level of perception, regardless of whether the teacher requests it or not. Upwards of ten panels per lecture are submitted by students for the instructor to privately confirm answers. The teacher can provide immediate feedback or save and return to the panels at a more convenient time. A feature that works particularly well for student personal reflection or portfolio is to request panels in response to probing questions. Student response to these activities is sometimes typed, or a combination of stylus written mathematical solution and typed explanation. The option of having both types of input at their fingertips gives students the choice to respond intuitively and contributes to their ability to express themselves freely. During each lecture, students search the Internet for definitions, interactive learning objects, applets, or tutorials, which are added into their notes for further reference. Using an online textbook resource, students capture questions and paste them directly into their notes to ink in solutions. Panels are a compilation of teacher examples, individual or group work, and collaborative class take-up and include all annotations, private notes, and Web sites, which are saved to a server maintained by the college. These notes are accessible to the student from anywhere, at any time, via the Internet, and provide the resource necessary for assignments and testing.

Attendance and assessment data are collected for both experimental and control groups. Survey response and focus groups are used to determine student perception of their engagement and learning. Based on the work of previous researchers [4, 6, 2], student opinion regarding the use of Tablet PC technology is collected in two parts in a survey of the experimental group after twelve weeks of instruction (current sample size is fifty-one). In the first part, students answer specific questions using a Likert scale of strongly agree, agree, neutral, disagree, and strongly disagree. Data is aggregated by combining strongly agree/agree as one category—positive (likewise with disagree/strongly disagree—negative). A response of neutral is kept as a single category as its meaning is difficult to interpret (no opinion, do not know, do not understand the question). In the second part, students are given the opportunity to respond to open-ended questions such as "What did you like best/least about having computers in the classroom?" Comments are analyzed using qualitative data analysis software (Atlas.ti). The open coding system [5] is used for initial analysis, and the constant comparative process [1] is used to group similarities and consistencies in the responses. Coded comments (918 in total) are associated into broad categories of attention/motivation, performance, learning, ease of access, and technology to give an indication as to which types of comments students make more frequently.

## 4. Evaluation

Initial results strongly suggest that Tablet PCs, in combination with interactive software, improve attendance, performance, group interaction, note taking skills, and the ability to have immediate teacher feedback, which students suggest results in increased engagement and enhanced learning. Data compiled for science classes provide similar evidence, although teaching methodology is somewhat different.

### 4.1 Impact on student engagement

**Figure 1.** Attendance data collected for mathematics groups.

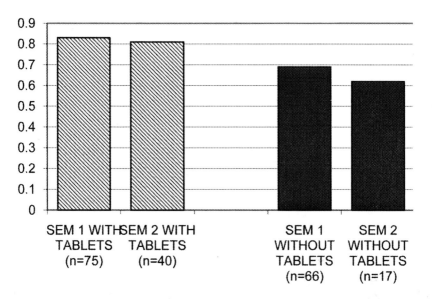

## % Attendance - MATH

The data in Figure 1 indicates the number of hours students attend class as a percentage of scheduled hours. When averaged over two semesters of math classes, the four cohorts of students using Tablet PCs attend more regularly (82 percent) versus students without Tablet PCs (68 percent). Attendance in the non-Tablet PC groups is 19 percent lower in second semester compared to the Tablet PC groups. Students in the Tablet PC group who attend class feel they are actively engaged in their course work as evidenced by an 80 percent postive (strongly agree/agree) response to the survey question "I paid more attention during lectures and class discussions" and 76 percent positive to "Having my work on the Tablet PC displayed for the class (shared control) improved my participation." In the open-ended response to questions such as "Explain whether the Tablet PCs helped you to perform better/worse on regular course assessments" or "Did the Tablet PCs influence you to attend class more often and persist through the end of the course in any way?," students gave 262 comments relating to the broad category of attention/motivation, of which 241 are positive. For example, 59 refer to the "positive class environment," 55 to "more enjoyable," 29 to "increased attendance," 25 to "class participation increased," and so on:

> "I really enjoyed using it, it helped get me to class. . . . I was excited to use the computer."

> "It isn't like any other class when you sit there and just listening to a teacher speak on and on . . . you're actually interacting with others."

> "By allowing students to lead the lecture and helping them . . ."

> "Tablet PCs . . . gave you an opportunity to participate . . . without the embarrassment of public speaking."

> "My participation . . . has grown significantly because of the confidence it brings when I'm comfortable of where I am."

> "It influences you because you're seeing not only your answers, but others' own as well, and it enables you to discuss different methods of solving problems."

As students often comment that they "aren't good at math" or "math is boring," to teach in an environment where students enjoy coming to class, want to participate, and are proud to display their work, although anecdotal, makes a far more rewarding teaching experience. From a teacher "We're all on DyKnow together. . . . it is kind of our forum where we meet and interact."

## 4.2 Impact on student learning and application of concepts

The results of a five-year study by the Ontario College Mathematics Project (CMP) found that 25 to 50 percent of first semester students either fail (F) or barely pass (D) math, which puts students at risk of not being able to complete their program of choice. Students who attain a grade of A+ to C are deemed to have "good grades" for the purpose of the CMP study [3]. In our study, of students using Tablet PCs, 71 percent (n = 75) in the first semester and 78 percent (n = 40) in the second semester have good grades. For students without Tablet PCs, the values are 64 percent (n = 66) and 59 percent (n = 17), respectively. Of interest, the largest groups to achieve good grades occur in the second semester Tablet PC classes, even though the material is more challenging and depends on a thorough understanding and application of foundational concepts. This trend is not observed in the groups without Tablet PCs. Perhaps the strong learning community that develops from the use of Tablet PCs and the interactive capabilities of the software give weaker students the confidence needed to persist to completion and be successful.

The survey item "The Tablet PC helped me improve my performance in this course" results in 74 percent of students responding positively. There were 274 comments relating to the broad category of "learning" in open-ended questions such as "Explain whether the Tablet PCs helped you to perform better/worse on regular course assessments including homework and tests." Of the 274 learning comments, 243 are coded as positive with reference made to "interaction in class improved" (50) and "improved learning" (47). Students like the fact that they could "share control" (27), "students teach" (16), "the teacher models approach to problem solving" (12), and a "better understanding of math processing" (15) is achieved; all necessary components of critical thinking:

> "I actually did my work and it was done right and organized..."

> ". . . because it's more convenient and accessible to everyone."

> "It made learning . . . much easier, more enjoyable, and improved my performance."

> "Makes me perform better since it is a new and interesting way to approach classes, I tend to pay attention more thus doing better in work and tests."

> "Helped me, as I haven't had a mark higher than B in a math class since grade 8, yet I am getting As here."

The software tool, DyKnow, provides a class environment of augmented cooperation and communication. Survey responses are 92 percent positive that "DyKnow was an effective tool for classroom presentations and note taking." Students have the opportunity to see not only the teachers' method of problem solving, but also the approach of other students (perhaps a more familiar one). It allows students to self-correct their work and determine for themselves the precise location of their error:

> "The Tablet PCs were useful because I can see what the teacher is writing, students can share answers anonymously, we can correct each other's work. Also by being able to access DyKnow at home and at school I did not have to worry about taking notes [on paper] because they were all saved."

The teacher has the opportunity to gauge student understanding far more effectively. "I would ask . . . if everyone was following along, and I'd get the occasional, 'yes,' 'no,' but, some students stayed quiet, and I wouldn't really know

if they would be understanding. If I asked the same question through . . . DyKnow
. . . I would see what those quiet students would be thinking. . . . It really helped
me target which students needed extra help."

Students respond to "What did you like least about having Tablet PCs in
the classroom?" that they sometimes found having the Tablet PCs could be distracting. Negative comments (103) about the technology are made relating to
the wireless connectivity, problems with technology, and slow class start. These
comments become more noted as the study progresses, perhaps indicating increasing tech-savvy of students, larger class sizes, aging equipment, or insuffi-
cient technology infrastructure. These issues continue to be addressed and require
further study.

### 4.3 Promotion of this teaching approach to other communities
Presentations and outreach activities are given at multiple forums and venues.
Often our demonstrations took the form of professional development workshops
with participants taking a hands-on approach. Teachers who are preparing to employ this type of student-centered instructional style should be comfortable with
the class working at multiple levels and at a pace that is largely determined by
student understanding. The teacher must be amenable to give students the opportunity to share their solutions with the rest of the class, and thus have students
contribute to the teaching role.

## 5. Future Work
In the fall of 2010 our college will increase the current Tablet PC classroom from
twenty to thirty-five seats and open a second, larger lab to accommodate forty
students. The aim is to determine the effect of increased class size on this enhanced use of technology practice. This will provide the necessary space required
to ensure that this learning style is transferable to a more common college class
size. Further, this methodology is being expanded to include additional courses
in developmental math and English.

## 6. Additional Resources
Hewlett-Packard Web site: http://open.senecac.on.ca/HPtabletproject/
WIPTE contest video: http://www.youtube.com/watch?v=il-k65CFqpE
DyKnow contest video: http://www.youtube.com/watch?v=Hd7BsEF1x6g

## 7. Acknowledgments
This work is supported by a 2008 Higher Education Hewlett-Packard Technology for Teaching Grant, a 2010 Post Secondary DyKnow Collaborative Grant,

and the Faculty of Applied Science and Engineering Technology and Enterprise Services Management at the college studied.

## References

[1] Glaser, B., and Strauss, A. *The discovery of grounded theory.* Aldine, Chicago, 1967.

[2] Moorehead State University. Assessment Statistics Calculus III Technology Survey. http://people2.morehead-st.edu/orgs/hpgrant/files/spring07survey.htm, accessed July 8, 2008.

[3] Orpwood, G., Schollen, L., Assiri, H., and Marinelli-Henriques, P. College Mathematics Project2009 Final Report. http://collegemathproject.senecac.on.ca.

[4] Rawat, K. S. Integrating HP Mobile Tablet PC Technology-Based Instruction Delivery System into Undergraduate Engineering Technology Courses. http://kultyrawat.com/project.htm, accessed July 8, 2008.

[5] Strauss, A., and Corbin, J. *Basics of qualitative research: Grounded theory procedures and techniques.* Sage, Newbury Park, 1990.

[6] Taylor, S., Takvorian, K. and Westover, D. Mount Wachusett Community College HP Technology for Teaching Grant Project. http://cisweb.mwcc.edu/st01/hpTabletProject/project.htm, accessed July 8, 2008.

# Implementing an Inverted Classroom Using Tablet PCs for Content Development

## Jeff Frolik,[1] Tom Weller,[2] Paul Flikkema,[3] and Carol Haden[4]

[1]University of Vermont, [2]University of South Florida, [3]Northern Arizona University, and [4]Magnolia Consulting

## 1. Abstract

This paper describes the development of a course for which multiple universities developed instructional videos using Tablet PCs and screen capture software. The videos were made available online and enabled the course instructors to implement an inverted classroom course structure. Students were assigned videos (i.e., the lectures) to watch outside of class while in-class time was spent elaborating on and applying the relevant concepts. Lessons learned from student and faculty evaluations are presented.

## 2. Problem Statement and Context

Multi-University Systems Education (MUSE) is an NSF-sponsored CCLI project that has been developing curricula emphasizing "systems thinking," a set of skills rarely taught in undergraduate engineering curricula, and only learned sporadically and informally in graduate school or industry. Systems thinking centers around the ability to conceive and design the complex engineered systems needed to address many of today's critical problems. Such systems require a broad range of expertise to develop and thus are truly interdisciplinary in scope. As such, to develop instructional material related to these systems, a diverse set of technical expertise is also required; a set that is often beyond the capabilities of a single institution.

The MUSE project has leveraged the technical expertise of faculty at multiple institutions to develop systems thinking skills in the context of wireless sensor networks (WSN). WSN directly incorporate almost every sub-discipline in electrical engineering, computer engineering, and computer science, from transducer technology to human interface design, and furthermore must be designed to meet a variety of operational constraints that vary by application (see Figure 1). The problem addressed in this paper is how to best collect and format content developed at multiple institutions and how to present it in a way that can be used by multiple institutions.

**Figure 1.** Wireless sensor networks as an example of a complex engineered system.

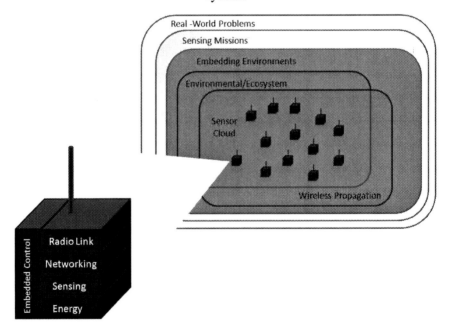

## 3. Solution Employed

Our objective was to offer students not only a course that emphasized systems thinking, but also to provide a learning experience that allows students to direct much of their learning by improving the utilization of time spent in the classroom. We employed an inverted classroom structure where lectures were held outside the classroom, and class time was used for extending course material and to work on experiments. Our lecture material consists of videos developed using Tablet PCs and screen capture software (TechSmith's Camtasia Studio). Three to seven (roughly) twenty-minute videos form modules of which there are ten that make up the course's video textbook: *Wireless Sensor Network Design* (Table 1).

**Table 1.** Table of contents for MUSE online video textbook.

| Module | Label | Module Title |
|--------|-------|--------------|
| 1 | [MOT] | Overview: Why Wireless Sensor Networks? |
| 2 | [SEA] | Systems Engineering Applied to WSN |
| 3 | [TDX] | Transducers |
| 4 | [ADC] | Analog-to-Digital Conversion |
| 5 | [EMC] | Managing the Sensor: Embedded Computing |
| 6 | [CTA] | Communication Theory Applied to WSN |
| 7 | [RFH] | Radio Frequency Hardware |
| 8 | [WCC] | The Wireless Communications Channel |
| 9 | [SNA] | Sensor Network Architectures |
| 10 | [FIN] | Bringing It All Together – Examples |

To develop a video, the instructor first creates a series of PowerPoint slides outlining the subject matter to be presented. These slides are saved as a Microsoft Journal document for subsequent inking (the project team found Journal inking to be much more responsive than PowerPoint, especially during screen capture). With the Journal document opened, a Camtasia screen capture window is set up and recording initiated. The recorded video captures both the inking of the Journal slide and the audio of the instructor discussing the content. As illustrated in Figures 2 through 4, inking enables images to be annotated, the dynamic development of equations, the use of different colors to highlight specific concepts, and so forth.

Once the slide discussion has been completed, the recording is stopped, a video clip saved, and the process repeats for the next slide of the document. Once all slides are recorded, the clips are brought into Camtasia Studio for video editing enabling the instructor to add title slides, a table of contents, quizzes (see Figure 4), or video clips from other sources. The resulting Camtasia project is rendered to a video format that best fits the instructor's needs and then uploaded to the course Web site. For example, to leverage the quiz feature, the rendering must be in Flash. However, to enable portability to iPad/iPod/iPhone, QuickTime is more appropriate.

## 4. Evaluation

To date, over twenty hours of content has been developed. The content was first utilized at Northern Arizona University (NAU) in fall 2008. During this offering, formative assessment was conducted through feedback surveys at the end of each week or two-week module. In the surveys, students were asked to rate individual modules for various aspects of quality and to respond to statements about how well the modules supported their learning of key course content. In addition to module surveys, student focus groups were conducted to gain a more in-depth understanding of student perceptions of module and course format and quality. Eleven students (of a total class size of seventeen) participated in data collection activities at NAU during the fall 2008 semester. These included ten males and one female, all of whom were senior undergraduates.

**Figure 2.** Example slide from a MUSE video module.

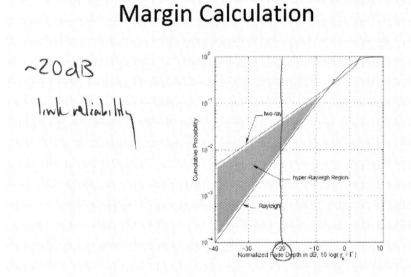

**Figure 3.** Slide fully developed with inking.

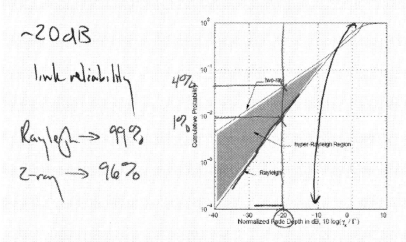

**Figure 4.** Embedded quiz enabled by Camtasia.

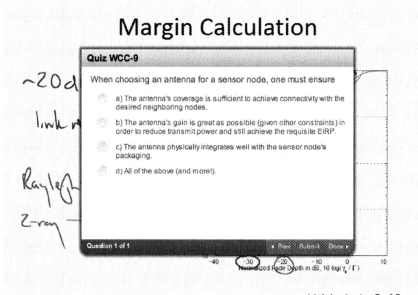

Results of the 2008 surveys and focus group interviews indicated that while students rated modules highly, there were issues with consistency and flow across modules. As noted, the course content was developed at three institutions. Furthermore, the modules were developed in parallel and thus students commented on inconsistencies in format, recording quality, among other issues. More importantly, the modules did not seem to tie in well to each other and thus did not adequately present a systems thinking approach.

Over the summer of 2009, these shortcomings were addressed with rerecording of some videos to improve the audio and content quality. In addition, new introductory videos were created for each module showing how the concepts to be covered relate to those in other modules. In each of these introductory clips, the image seen in Figure 1 was used to reinforce understanding of systems thinking.

In fall 2009, the course was offered at NAU and the University of Vermont (UVM). Twenty-seven students across the two institutions participated in data collection activities during the fall 2009 semester. These included fourteen undergraduates and thirteen graduate students of whom twenty-four were male and three were female. Students in this cohort completed the same module feedback surveys as those in the 2008 cohort. Additionally, students at both institutions participated in focus group interviews. Some key findings comparing the fall 2009 offering to the fall 2008 are as follows.

On the module feedback surveys, students rated each module on the quality of format, organization, pace, and graphics on a five-point scale (1 = Poor, 2= Fair, 3 = Average, 4 = Good, 5 = Excellent). Students also rated each module for overall quality. Mean ratings across modules were compared from the fall 2008 offering to the fall 2009 offering. Figure 5 presents the results of these comparisons.

Ratings across all modules increased from the fall 2008 offering to the fall 2009 offering on all aspects including organization, graphics, format, pace, and overall quality. Three increases were statistically significant at the .05 alpha level. Ratings of module organization were significantly higher in fall 2009 (M = 4.27, SD = .776) than in fall 2008 (M = 4.00, SD = .697); t (223) = 2.57, p = .008. Ratings of module format were significantly higher in fall 2009 (M = 4.32, SD = .677) than in fall 2008 (M = 3.93, SD = .811); t (225) = 3.81, p < .0001. And finally, ratings of overall module quality were significantly higher in fall 2009 (M = 4.22, SD = .721) than in fall 2008 (M = 3.87, SD = .859); t (225) = 3.29, p = .001. These findings suggest that the revisions to the modules enhanced their quality and improved student learning.

As compared to the fall 2008 cohort, students in the fall 2009 cohort indicated that the revised modules were highly effective in helping them to under-

**Figure 5.** Fall 2008 and fall 2009 ratings across modules.

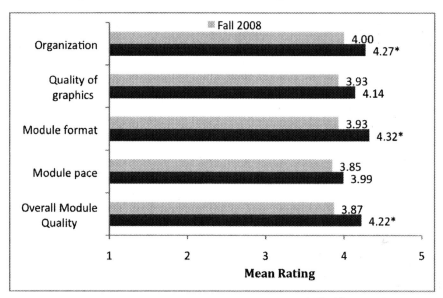

* Significant at the .05 level

stand the concept of systems thinking in engineering. They noted that systems thinking was made overt through the modules and the ways in which they flowed together and built upon one another. Students commented that they thought of the course as a "systems engineering course that happens to be focused on wireless networks."

Across both cohorts, the inverted classroom format was new to all students. In both cohorts, the students appreciated the ability to watch the videos on their own time and the fact that they could be viewed anywhere. Students commented that they liked the inverted format for the online videos because it created a "self-paced" nature for the course (students typically had a week to watch an assigned set of videos and answer wiki questions). They also liked the ability of going back over the video to review material, something "you can't do in class."

Students noted that the video format means that the faculty members are not immediately available to answer specific questions. One student commented, "In class, a professor can see when students are not getting something." In short, the videos are not interactive. To address this negative aspect of the inverted class-room format, a wiki was utilized at UVM. For each module, a wiki page that was seeded with questions developed by the instructor was also made available for students to post their own questions.

The modular nature of the developed course has enabled other institutions to utilize the developed content on an ad hoc basis by integrating selected modules into an existing course to show applications of the topics. To date, content has been incorporated in to a variety of courses at the University of Hawaii, University of Minnesota, University of Utah, and University of South Florida.

Feedback was collected through interviews with instructors at the University of Minnesota and University of Hawaii at the end of the fall 2009 and fall 2010 semesters. Instructors indicated that the online video modules were useful to plug into existing courses where appropriate. They appreciated the flexibility in the use of the modules to either support content they were already teaching or to supplement and "provide a different perspective" on their own course content. Instructors also noted that the MUSE modules were effective in helping to show a systems approach to engineering. They noted the need for an "Instructor page" on the MUSE Web site to provide a map for how modules might fit into existing courses and also the need for more extensive homework problems associated with the modules.

## 5. Future Work

The MUSE modules are currently being rendered to a QuickTime format to enable additional dissemination through iTunesU and use on iPods and iPads. An adoption guide (i.e., "Instructors page") has been developed to guide faculty in incorporating the content in existing courses. In addition, we are looking to expand the course modules to include topics such as energy harvesting, biomedical applications, and microsatellites to different curricular areas such as environmental engineering.

## 6. Additional Resources

The reader is encouraged to explore the "Wireless Sensor Network Design" course content online at the MUSE project Web site: www.uvm.edu/~muse. Additional reports and assessment on this project have been presented at FIE 2008 [3], ASEE 2009 [4], ASEE 2010 [1], and FIE 2010 [2].

## 7. Acknowledgments

This work was supported by NSF Grant DUE-0717326.

## References

[1] Flikkema, P., Weller, T., Frolik, J., and Haden, C. Experiential learning of complex engineered systems in the context of wireless sensor networks. *2010 ASEE Annual Conference*, Louisville, KY, June 20-23.

[2] Flikkema, P., Franklin, R., Frolik, J., Haden, C., Shiroma, W., and Weller, T. MUSE—Multi-University Systems Education Mini-Workshop, *FIE 2010*. Washington DC, October 27-30.

[3] Frolik, J., Weller, T., Flikkema, P., and Shiroma, W. Work in Progress: MUSE—Multi-University Systems Education, *FIE 2008*. Saratoga Springs, NY, October 22-25.

[4] Haden, C., Flikkema, P., Weller, T., Frolik, J., Verrei-Berenback, W., and Shiroma, W. Assessment of a hybrid, online/in-class course developed at multiple universities. *2009 ASEE Annual Conference*. Austin, TX, June 14-17.

# Using Tablet PCs and Pen-based Technology to Address Poor Student Performance in an Engineering Technology Class

*Robert D. Garrick and Marybeth Koon*

*Rochester Institute of Technology*

## 1. Abstract

Rochester Institute of Technology offers a Pneumatics and Hydraulics lecture and laboratory class each year, and experience has shown that most students perform well in this class. However, some students struggle and receive a low grade or withdraw from the class. To address the issue of poor student performance, a structured experiment was conducted to evaluate the use of Tablet PC digital ink technology in a lecture format. The objective of this experiment was to assess how Tablet PCs could help improve student learning. To minimize variation, the class was arranged during one term to be taught with one weekly lecture in a standard lecture environment and one weekly lecture using DyKnow software and Tablet PCs. Previous experience within the department indicated that Tablet PCs and improved note taking can greatly help students who do poorly. This mixed-methods evaluation utilizes an experimental design that minimizes variation by studying one group of students, one class section, and one instructor to better isolate the effects of DyKnow/Tablet PC usage. Student attitude surveys, a student focus group, and outside observations performed by a teaching and learning professional in both the standard lecture and DyKnow/Tablet PC environments were the methods utilized to gather rich qualitative and quantitative data.

## 2. Problem Statement and Context

Pneumatics and Hydraulics is offered at Rochester Institute of Technology (RIT) to second year students, and the course frequently has a high rate of low grades or students withdrawing from the class. The percent of students receiving a grade of D or F, along with students withdrawing from the class has averaged 22.8 percent over the last ten quarters (five years and two classes per year) the class was taught. The total number of students taking this class over this period was 504 students. With a 22.8 percent D, W, or F rate, approximately 115 students would have to repeat the class or withdraw from the program. This large number affects the department's retention rate and class scheduling.

A previous study within the RIT Department of Mechanical and Manufacturing Engineering Technology demonstrated that Tablet PC-based lectures helped students who had lower GPAs to a greater extent than those with higher GPAs [1]. Students with a lower GPA benefited by receiving additional notes as a supplement to the general outline presentation. Using a Tablet PC lecture environment has also been reported to increase student interest and involvement in engineering and science classroom studies [2-9]. The selection of a Tablet PC learning environment was chosen for the Pneumatics and Hydraulics class due to the highly visual and practical application in the material. The objective in using Tablet PCs with multimedia lectures would allow the students to see the connections between equations, real world applications, and the laboratory experiments. A single class ($n = 27$) was selected as the experimental group with students having the same background as previous classes (no changes in prerequisites, GPA requirements, background, etc.) during the five year study period.

## 3. Solution Employed and Experiment Design

With any change in lecture delivery a careful analysis must be completed to assure that the change in delivery, and not another uncontrolled factor, caused the desired effect. Therefore, to assess the change from a traditional lecture method to a Tablet PC/DyKnow lecture environment for the Pneumatics and Hydraulics class, the lectures were delivered in alternating learning environments. The class lectures were scheduled twice per week (Tuesday and Thursday) for two hours each, and alternated during the entire class term with one lecture (Tuesday) delivered in a computer lab and one lecture (Thursday) delivered in a Tablet PC/DyKnow lab. During the Tuesday computer lab lecture, each student would have access to a computer with the instructor's prepared lecture notes (PowerPoint) available. This would allow students to take notes either using pen and paper or typed computer notes. For each class a group problem solving and individual problem solving quiz was administered. In the Tuesday computer lab environment the group problem solving exercise was difficult with students having to move into groups around one workstation, and was therefore discontinued midterm due to the class disruption. The individual quiz was administered using a traditional pen and paper method in this environment. During the other weekly lecture (Thursday) in the Tablet PC/DyKnow lab, each student would have a Tablet PC and the full capabilities of digital ink technology. This Tablet PC environment allowed the students to take pen and paper, typed, or digital ink notes over the instructor's prepared lecture notes. The group problem solving exercise was easily accomplished using pre-loaded groups and did not require students to move locations, but allowed them to collaborate on shared screens. The group solved problems were able to be retrieved and reviewed in the class using the capabilities of DyKnow. Individual quizzes were included electronically in the prepared notes and retrieved, graded, and returned electronically. Both lectures were delivered by the same instructor during the entire term using PowerPoint animation and external videos where appropriate, so that the material for each lecture was as similar as possible. Both lectures provided computer usage for each student so that the effect of having a computer was not confounded with the lecture delivery utilizing Tablet PCs/DyKnow. This experimental design allowed the single student study group population to be exposed to the two different lecture environments over the entire quarter to allow the students to assess the impact of the different environments on their learning. An external instructional design specialist observed classes in both settings to provide an additional evaluation source.

## 4. Evaluations

The evaluation of the Tablet PC/DyKnow-based lecture as compared to the computer lab lecture consisted of four parts. The first evaluation of the two lecture formats was conducted by an independent instructional designer from the RIT Teaching and Learning Center. The instructional designer observed multiple lectures in each setting with the following observations. Two observations took place during the Tuesday class, which was held in a more traditional computer lab, and two observations took place in the Tablet PC/DyKnow studio. In her observations, she attempted to make comparisons between those variables and activities that were "constants" in both of these classrooms, each with different layouts and equipment. The variables and activities she focused on in particular were desk and computer set up, projection of lecture material, content-specific examples, note-taking activity, and student engagement.

The professor was interested in learning if these observations would provide data on whether or not the different layout and equipment available in these classrooms, in combination with changes he made to his instructional approach, had a noticeable impact on student engagement and performance. The most significant difference in instructional approach was the implementation of a collaborative software, called DyKnow, and use of a three-screen display in the Tablet PC studio during the Thursday class. During the Tuesday class, the instructor used the same instructional approach as he had used in the past.

### 4.1.1 Instruction Designer Review—Lecture and Course Content Display

In the Tuesday session, the instructor carried out his lecture in the manner in which he had done so before. He would deliver a lecture on new material in the form of a PowerPoint that was projected onto the single screen. During the lecture, he would incorporate breaks into his lecture for some review of the concepts with students. This review usually consisted of an activity whereby the instructor would work out an example up at the whiteboard while the students would follow along by watching, some opting to take notes. In some cases, his PowerPoint would have step-by-step animations that he would click through to also demonstrate these examples. In these situations, most students seemed to passively watch the lecture up at the front of the class or follow along at the computer where they would have the lecture also displayed.

In the Thursday session, the instructor planned his instruction differently based on the equipment and software that was available in the Tablet PC studio. The most significant change in his approach in the Thursday class was his use of DyKnow, a collaborative program, which enabled him and the students to have an integrated resource consisting of the PowerPoint lecture and real-time annotations and notes that both he and the students could incorporate during the live lecture. This material could then be saved and housed on a server for students to access for review at a later time. Although the instructor's annotations and notes would be viewable to all students in the session, any notes that the individual students would take during the session were only viewable to them. With the option of the three-screen display in the Tablet PC studio, the instructor also projected two PowerPoint slides at one time. Because both the instructor and students were logged into this DyKnow session, students had the option of following along by watching the screens at the front of the class or following along directly from their Tablet PCs.

### 4.1.2 Instruction Designer Review—Content-Specific Examples

With the use of DyKnow to incorporate in-class activities in the Thursday session, students seemed much more engaged in the exercises and more vocal during the review process that followed. There was generally a "din" of discussion and commentary that would emerge among the students and the instructor as they worked out the examples and diagrams. In addition, the process of submitting the work and having it displayed for review by all seemed to provide more chances for students to see how others solved the problem and not just how the instructor completed the work. Based on the classroom layout, seating configuration, and use of DyKnow and the Tablet PCs, students had more options for viewing the material being presented, completed, and reviewed than they did when limited to just the dry-erase whiteboard and single-screen projection in the Tuesday class.

### 4.1.3 Instruction Designer Review—Student Engagement

The tendency observed of students surfing the Web, accessing e-mail, or sites like Facebook seemed to be about equal in both Tuesday and Thursday sessions while the instructor lectured. The likelihood of this happening did not seem any more or less likely to occur in one classroom environment over the other. However, I did notice that as soon as the instructor called the students' attention to an in-class activity within DyKnow, it did seem to "pull" those students back into the lecture content and the in-class activity. At least two students were observed looking at other Web sites and immediately switch back to the DyKnow session as soon as the instructor announced it was time for the in-class activity due to the need to utilize the Tablet PC for the activity. In comparison, during the lecture without the Tablet PC/DyKnow environment the activities were paper-based and students at times remained distracted or tried to multitask between the paper and Web site they were accessing. The Tablet PC/DyKnow environment appeared more effective in pulling the students back into the lecture.

### 4.2 End-of-Class Student Survey

The second evaluation format consisted of an end-of-class student survey comparing the two lecture environments and the features of each classroom. Students were asked about how they usually take notes in a non-Tablet PC environment. Seventy-eight percent of the students reported that they typically take notes using a pen and paper method previous to the use of Tablet PCs. Students were then asked about their preferred lecture delivery style using a five-point Likert scale. From this survey it seems students prefer a multi-dimensional lecture with both a visual and audio presentation of the material. The lecture preferences included the ability for example problem completion by both the instructor and by groups. The completion of group work was preferred to individual work. This preference may represent the ability of group work to provide peer-to-peer instructional opportunities, along with the experiential learning opportunity of solving problems.

The students rated the features of a classroom that they felt were the most important on a five-point Likert scale (unimportant, little importance, moderate importance, important, very important). They rated the abilities of receiving instructor written notes along with student notes on prepared PowerPoint lecture presentation slides as important/very important. The features of having desktop computers and flexibility of seating arrangements were of lower importance. The students reported in an approximate 2:1 ratio that the Tablet PC/DyKnow lecture environment made them more likely to take notes and use these notes for both homework and pre-test reviews. They felt again with an approximate 2:1 ratio that the notes taken in this lecture environment were more thorough and helped them better in the comprehension of the material.

The students ranked how solving problems in class using the Tablet PC/DyKnow environment helped them learn the material. They felt with a greater than 90 percent agree/strongly agree ratio that completing exercises as individuals and in a group format helped them learn the material better than just watching the instructor complete problems. They overwhelming agreed that working virtually in groups with the Tablet PC/DyKnow format was an effective method to solving these in-class problems. Overall, the students recommended the Tablet PC/DyKnow lecture environment with a 94 percent agree/strongly agree for this Pneumatics and Hydraulics class. They also responded with a high preference for the Tablet PC environment over the standard computer lab environment for lectures.

## 4.3 Student Focus Group

The third evaluation technique consisted of a focus group of the students in the Pneumatics and Hydraulics class. This focus group was lead by an external evaluator experienced in facilitating focus groups and lasted thirty minutes. The focus group was videotaped and transcribed for analysis. The common theme among the students was a strong preference for group work due to being able to learn from peers and the low stress nature of working with peers to solve problems. The students also commented about the how the different environments affected their note taking: "If you're taking notes down, you're more worried about copying down what he's writing instead of actually looking at what he's doing and understanding more." Students commented that when using notes for homework or tests, "I found myself going to the saved documents on DyKnow to go through the notes." An overall theme from the focus group was that the students felt that the Tablet PC/DyKnow lecture environment can be very helpful for student learning when used by an instructor skilled in the technology and in teaching.

## 4.4 Student Performance

The fourth evaluation technique consisted of students' performance using similar test questions, homework assignments, and quizzes as compared to previous classes. Previous classes were offered using the same number of contact hours per week as the Tablet PC/DyKnow test group, and included specific time during the contact hours for students to solve problems and receive instructor feedback during a recitation period. This recitation period was conducted in a computer laboratory with each student having a computer and students having the ability to work in ad-hoc groups. Since the previous classes did not have DyKnow or Tablet PCs, the group work was not as formal or collaborative. All students in the Table PC/DyKnow experiment group (n = 27) achieved an A, B, or C grade (no D, W, or F students) compared to the historical 22.8 percent D, W, or F rate for this class. With this historical failure rate over this sample size one could expect approximately six D, W, or F students from the experimental group. Since the experimental group had zero D, W, or F students, from a Poisson distribution we would have a 99 percent confidence that this experiment sample is different from the previous population in terms of class performance.

## 5. Future Work

To expand on this initial study the faculty who teach this class will be offering, during the 2010-2011 academic year, the class lectures in this "blended" computer lab-Tablet PC/DyKnow learning environment. This expanded study will increase the population of students involved in the experiment to greater than one hundred and allow a more statistically significant analysis of student performance using similar test questions, homework assignments, and quizzes as compared to previous classes.

## References

[1] Parthum, M. Teaching with a Tablet PC, a new technology for the classroom and academic usage. In *2009 ASEE Annual Conference and Exposition*. Austin, TX, June 14-17, 2009.

[2] Birmingham, W., DiStasi, V., and Welton, G. Learning style, student motivation, and active learning. In *2009 ASEE Annual Conference and Exposition*. Austin, TX, June 14-17, 2009.

[3] Chidanandan, A., et al. Work in progress—Assessing the impact of penbased computing and collaboration-facilitating software in the classroom. In *37th ASEE/IEEE Frontiers in Education Conference, FIE*. Milwaukee, WI, Oct. 10- 13, 2007, T1G17-T1G18.

[4] Chidanandan, A., et al. Panel session—pen-based computing in the engineering and Science Classroom: Implementation scenarios from three institutions. In *38th ASEE/IEEE Frontiers in Education Conference, FIE.* Saratoga Springs, NY, Oct. 22-25, 2008, F4G1-F4G2.

[5] Johri, A., and Lohani, V. Representational literacy and participatory learning in large engineering classes using pen-based computing. In *2008 IEEE Frontiers in Education Conference.* Piscataway, NJ, Oct. 22-25, 2008, 6.

[6] Lohani, V., Castles, R., Johri, A., Spangler, D., and Kibler, D. Analysis of Tablet PC based learning experiences in freshman to junior level engineering courses. In *2008 ASEE Annual Conference and Exposition.* Pittsburg, PA, June 22-24, 2008.

[7] Sneller, J. The Tablet PC classroom: erasing borders, stimulating activity, enhancing communication. In *37th Annual Frontiers in Education Conference—Global Engineering: Knowledge Without Borders, Opportunities Without Passports.* Piscataway, NJ, Oct. 10-13, 2007, 3-5.

[8] Stanton, K. Work in progress—Enhancement of problem solving techniques with Tablet PC-based learning technologies. In *38th ASEE/IEEE Frontiers in Education Conference, FIE,* Saratoga Springs, NY, Oct. 22-25, 2008, S4D25-S4D26.

[9] Berque, D., Johnson, D. K., and Jovanovic, L. Teaching theory of computation using pen-based computers and an electronic whiteboard. In *Proceedings of the 6th Annual SIGCSE Conference on Innovation and Technology in Computer Science Education.* Cantenbury, United Kingdom, June 25-27, 2001, 169-172.

# An Attitudinal Study of Pen Technology and Web-based Recordings to Accommodate Students with Disabilities in Post-Secondary Science, Technology, Engineering, and Math Courses

*Laura Graves and Stacey Plant*

*Tennessee Technological University*

## 1. Abstract

This paper presents an attitudinal study of students with learning disabilities (SWLD) at four post-secondary institutions as part of a larger National Science Foundation research study. Students attended at least one science, technology, engineering, or mathematics (STEM) course where instructors used digital pen technology as the platform for delivering course content in the classroom. This content was recorded through screen and audio capture technology that allowed asynchronous Web access. The solution employed strives to meet equitable use among all students. Six overall common themes emerged from the transcribed interviews: clarity, organization, asynchronous access, convenience, achievement, and coping mechanisms. Focus group questions reflected access, usage, attitude toward Web-based recordings, and attitude toward perceived achievement and learning in STEM courses by SWLD.

## 2. Problem Statement and Context

Obtaining a degree from a post-secondary institution has become an attainable goal for many students. Unfortunately, SWLD may be denied reasonable access by the manner in which coursework is presented [2]. SWLD, including students with attention deficit disorder (ADD) and attention deficit hyperactivity disorder (ADHD), may be required to focus on teaching methods that are contrary to their learning strengths [3]. When this occurs, students may be forced to take notes rapidly which may interfere with their ability to focus on listening, or may be asked to focus on auditory processing tasks when their strength lies in mnemonic representations. This limitation may be considered a form of exclusion for SWLD since they do not have the same access to a successful post-secondary education as compared to their non-disabled peers. The Americans with Disabilities Act of 1990 prohibits any public agency, including universities, from denying access to individuals with disabilities while allowing access to those without disabilities [1].

Designing an inclusive environment using digital pen technology to deliver content for diverse populations utilizes Universal Design (UD) as its foundation; "UD promotes an expanded goal to make products and environments welcoming and useful to groups that are diverse in many dimensions, including gender, race and ethnicity, age, socio-economic status, ability, disability, and learning styles" [2]. This increases all students' accessibility and usability asynchronously, while decreasing the need for specific accommodations such as note-takers or tape recorded lectures. UD also meets the needs of the community of learners while focusing on access for all learners. UD is "engineered for flexibility and designed to anticipate the need for alternatives, options, and adaptations to meet the challenge of diversity" [4]. Accessible pedagogy through multiple means of representation, expression, and engagement are the cornerstone of UD for learning [4]. UD for learning also allows SWLD to "disappear" into the general population, becoming invisible or unidentifiable as compared to their non-disabled peers [5].

The National Science Foundation awarded Tennessee Technological University (TTU) a research grant in disability education (Award #0726449) in June 2007 titled "The Effects of Teaching with Tablet PCs with Asynchronous Student Access in Post-Secondary STEM Courses on Students with Learning Disabilities (TTASA-SWLD)." TTASA-SWLD analyzed attitudes toward science, technology, engineering, and math (STEM) courses at the post-secondary level, academic success in STEM courses, and academic persistence. For the purpose of the study, learning disabilities included ADD, ADHD, or any other cognitive disorder such as dysgraphia, dyscalculia, or dyslexia. TTU had three partnering institutions: Tennessee State University (TSU), Nashville State Community College (NSCC—a historically black university), and Roane State

Community College (RSCC), all located within the state of Tennessee. A total of twenty-four SWLD participated in the STEM experimental sections and twenty SWLD participated in STEM control sections of TTASA-SWLD. Of the twenty-four SWLD in experimental sections, eleven SWLD were interviewed and four SWLD participated in the focus group. SWLD self-disclose through the Office of Disability Services (ODS). On TTU's campus from spring 2008 through fall 2009 there were a total of thirty-four students with learning disabilities and forty-one students with ADD/ADHD registered through the ODS. TTU's total enrollment of all students each semester (fall/spring) is approximately ten thousand.

## 3. Solution Employed

In keeping with the objective described by UD, the accommodation employed for this research was primarily the Tablet PC and its digital version of a whiteboard and pen technology, specifically Microsoft Windows Journal. The digital whiteboard does not hold the same constraints of the traditional classroom whiteboard. An unlimited number of digital whiteboards can be prepared before class and accessed as individual or comprehensive files, eliminating the need to recycle each. The recording of live digitally annotated content allows for full retrieval not to exclude the chronological process of problem solving in STEM-related courses. This is crucial when dealing with STEM courses that heavily rely on complicated and lengthy equations, intricately detailed experimentation, and a large array of terminology.

This solution meets UD and strives to meet equitable use among all students with alternative means of access for the same content delivered. In the opinion of the researchers, the nature of the traditional classroom lends itself to a stress-filled environment for SWLD. This magnifies their need to filter a multitude of auditory and sensory inputs. This may limit the intake of purposed course content. Continuous access to delivered content allows students to employ their personal learning strengths in class instead of concentrating on their learning based upon their current set of weaknesses.

The initial platform used for recording was ElluminateLive. This software application incorporates live Internet streaming of video computer screen capturing and audio recording resulting in a generated link for access. The ElluminateLive software is required for viewing generated recording files. Technology representatives for the grant discovered and employed an alternative method for lecture capture recording. The discovered software application was Camtasia Relay. This software streamlined recording producing in MP4 format for easy playback. Both software applications allowed full video player features including play, stop, pause, fast-forward, and rewind capabilities.

Technology representatives conducted a workshop for training the fourteen faculty who participated in the experimental research prior to each semester. This training incorporated basic digital pen input panel functions, Microsoft Windows Journal, and Microsoft Office Annotation training, and either ElluminateLive or Camtasia Relay procedures. STEM courses represented in this research were Biology 1010, 1120, and 2020; Chemistry 1120 and 1110; and Math 1130, 1530, and 1910.

## 4. Evaluation

A total of eleven students enrolled in ten different sections of STEM courses were interviewed over four semesters. TTASA-SWLD interviews were conducted and evaluated by external qualitative researchers. A student participant focus group was conducted at the end of fall 2009. The focus group consisted of three students in experimental math sections and one student in an experimental chemistry section.

### 4.1 TTASA-SWLD Interview Question Finding Summary

Eleven SWLD taking STEM courses with accommodation of the Tablet PC digital whiteboard and pen technology were interviewed. The semi-structured interviews were digitally recorded and notes were taken to capture non-verbal cues. To better interpret the data collected during interviews, the recordings were transcribed verbatim and analyzed using line-by-line coding and data reduction. Six overall themes emerged: clarity, organization, asynchronous access/technical know-how, convenience, achievement, and disability coping mechanism.

- *Clarity:* Student participants found viewing the digital pen enabled whiteboard asynchronously reduced irregularities in their own note taking as well as improved comprehension of course content. Participants indicated the impact on learning had a positive overall effect of their perception of STEM-related courses.

- *Organization:* Most student participants found the accommodation to be presented in a systematic manner and led to a smooth transition during study time. Once accessed, the overall design of captured lectures and classroom activity delivered though digital pen inking on a digital whiteboard allowed for better understanding. The organization of learning materials helped student participants to prepare and study for exams in a systematic manner.

- *Asynchronous Access/Technical Know-How:* Student participants suggested the success of the accommodation were dependent on the instructor's ability to understand and know how to use the technology. Variables such as background noise, inexperience of instructor in use of technology, bandwidth strength of participant's network access when using ElluminateLive, instructor's voice not synchronized with visual presentation, and problems accessing recordings led to frustration by participants.

• *Convenience:* Student participants found the accommodation provided a practical systematic approach to learning for SWLD. Participants liked the availability of class lectures that met their needs based on when and where they wanted to study. Participants could work independently at their own pace and therefore did not feel time constraints as experienced in a typical post-secondary classroom. Participants liked not having to ask questions of the instructor or their friends; instead they were able to view digital whiteboard activity with audio as many times as was necessary in order to better learn the material.

• *Achievement:* Student participants found the accommodation of Web-based recordings enabled them to pursue a higher grade. Participants found recordings allowed them to review materials without approaching the professor with questions. This experience has encouraged participants to seek and enroll in more classes using digital pen technology and Web-based recordings.

• *Disability Coping Mechanism:* Participants suggested that they were able to use their learning strengths during class instead of focusing on their weaknesses in note taking and listening. Rather than being forced to engage in auditory processing, students indicated they were able to focus on visual representations of course materials while in class. Concepts were re-enforced when participants accessed Web-based recordings to navigate at their own pace in place of traditional textbook learning.

• *Summary:* SWLD participants found asynchronous access to Tablet PC whiteboard content useful in helping them learn course material in the STEM disciplines. Participants found the material organized, and the program led to a feeling of independence.

## 4.2. TTASA-SWLD Focus Group Finding Summary

Focus group questions reflected access, usage, and attitude toward Web-based recordings and attitude toward perceived achievement and learning in STEM courses by SWLD. Student responses indicated confusion between understanding the Web-based recordings and other Web-based materials instructors posted. Of the four students, three accessed the digital pen inking Web-based recordings at least once during the fall semester. One student reported using an audio-recorder during class (as an accommodation) and therefore did not feel he needed to access the Web-based recordings.

*4.2.1 Access:* Students reported knowing how to access recordings but also reported long download times and problems accessing recordings online. According to students, poor microphone audio limited usable access of the Web-based recordings. Although they could view the recording, the audio was either limited or nonexistent. Students also reported a decrease in attendance rates when the instructor provided access to digital pen technology and Web-based recordings. Students reported such access as a helpful accommodation for their specific learning disability.

*4.2.2 Usage:* Students accessed the recordings when absent from class or when they needed to study for a test. Students reported a potential to learn more when using the recordings to build on learning strengths (visual, auditory, kinesthetic, etc.).

*4.2.3. Attitude toward STEM courses:* Students recommended access to Web-based recordings in STEM courses as a beneficial accommodation. If given a choice, students would enroll in future STEM courses using digital pen technology and Web-based recordings as opposed to STEM courses not using these tools. Student attitude toward educational major remained consistent. Of the four students, three are majoring in engineering and one in business.

## 4.3. Limitations of Study

Technology advancements that optimize available solutions evolve rapidly. The need for recorded digital whiteboard content delivery is met but not without some limitations. Informal faculty interviews indicated that the ElluminateLive recording feature was moderately successful at the onset of this research and improved as streamlined lecture capture technology with Camtasia Relay emerged to provide a better user experience. Participants also found the overall technology or use of technology was in need of some improvements. Where the projected digital whiteboard and pen technology succeeded to bring greater clarity of content in the classroom, the recording capability lacks reliability hindering the anticipated benefits to SWLD. Caution should be used when generalizing data results to other post-secondary institutions using pen technology and asynchronous access as an accommodation due to low participant numbers.

## 5. Contributions and Future Work

The TTASA-SWLD project has provided the Office of Disabilities Services (ODS) with an alternative, universally designed accommodation for SWLD that had not been considered before. At the post-secondary level, many SWLD do not self-disclose through the ODS. While this makes it difficult in terms of the project, SWLD may still enroll in the courses using the accommodation of Web-based access to digitally annotated content. Furthermore, students without disabilities may profit from the same accommodation SWLD benefit from while neither group is disclosed.

The TTASA-SWLD trainings were attended by STEM faculty, ODS staff, personnel from the Academic/Administrative Offices, and members of the technology support teams. The TTASA-SWLD project has increased communication between diverse groups on each participating campus. It has also increased awareness of alternate approaches to accommodate learning needs of SWLD as well as broaden the understanding of universal design in post-secondary education.

Sustainability of the accommodation will continue with the use of the eighteen Tablet PC computers in STEM courses including developmental math courses. The Dell server purchased with grant funds has been transferred to the Technology Institute. In collaboration with the Technology Institute, future training for the Tablet PC will also include disability education.

## 6. Additional Resources

Plant, Stacey (2009, January 12). NSF award #0726449 Effects of Teaching with Tablet PCs with Asynchronous Student Access in Post-Secondary STEM Courses on Students with Learning Disabilities. http://www.tntech.edu/ttasa-swld/ttasa/, accessed April 2009.

National Science Foundation: Research in Disability Education. Available from http://www.nsf.gov/funding/pgm_summ.jsp?pims_id=5482.

Virtual Classroom Software (Version 8.0.0) [ElluminateLive]. Available from http://www.elluminate.com/products/index.jsp.

Automated Presentation and Lecture Capture (Version 1.0.0) [Camtasia Relay]. Available from http://www.techsmith.com/camtasiarelay.asp.

## References

[1] Americans with Disabilities Act of 1990, Pub. L. No. 101-336, § 2, 104 Stat. 328 (1991).

[2] Burgstahler, S. E. Universal Design in Higher Education. In S. E. Burstahler and R. C. Cory (Eds.), *Universal design in higher education: From principles to practice.* Harvard Education Press, Cambridge, MA, 2008, 3-20.

[3] Gardner, H. *Frames of mind.* Basic Books, New York, 1983.

[4] Rose, D. H., Harbour, W. S., Johnston, C. S., Daley, S. G., and Abardanell, L. Universal design for learning in post-secondary education: Reflections on principles and their application. In S. E. Burstahler and R. C. Cory (Eds.), *Universal design in higher education: From principles to practice.* Harvard Education Press, Cambridge, MA, 2008, 45-72.

[5]  Winick, S. L., and Gomez, C. (Eds.). *Disability compliance for higher education: 2008 year book.* LRP Publications, Horsham, PA, 2008.

# Tablet Computing, Creativity, and Teachers as Applied Microgenetic Analysts: A Paradigm Shift in Math Teacher Professional Development

*Eric Hamilton and Nancy Harding*

*Pepperdine University*

## 1. Abstract

This effort is funded by the Institute for Education Sciences (IES) [1] and the National Science Foundation (NSF) [2]. It advances a vision for personalized learning communities in mathematics education. Tablet PC computing provides entrée to naturalistic handwriting and symbolic notation at the core of mathematical manipulation in K-16 and graduate learning in mathematics. The project uses this affordance to help teachers customize instruction through development of video libraries that require freehand mathematical notation and drawing. It directs teachers to what can be considered the intersection of student cognition, mathematical content, and interactive digital media. The work bridges eclectic theoretical perspectives, while leveraging Tablet PCs functioning in tandem with screen-imaging software. Teacher interviews suggest multiple advances in professional development.

## 2. Problem Statement

This project arises out of three somewhat unrelated needs in mathematics education. These needs jointly lend themselves to novel solutions through engaging teachers in Tablet PC-enabled professional development

*Need 1: Internet-accessible digital library resources are difficult to use.* The first need involves the limited usability in classroom and private study settings of Internet-accessible digital resources for mathematics learning. Ironically, the largest single investor in digital content infrastructure, the National Science Foundation's NSDL Program [3], outlines this deficiency succinctly: "It is often difficult to determine from a lengthy list of links how well an individual item suits a particular learner's needs. When resources are located, they can exhibit uneven reliability or stability particularly if they incorporate additional software elements for animations, audio, or video. In addition, the audience for these collections often lacks the support and expertise needed to select an appropriate resource, incorporate it into a coherent learning experience, and evaluate the impact of the new approach" (2). The breadth and depth of the NSDL linked repositories are not yet matched by use or impact.

*Need 2: Deficiencies in professional development and status of teachers.* A second need this effort addresses is professional growth and the declining status of mathematics teachers in the current high-stakes testing environments that now define state and federal K-12 education policies [4]. Current policies respond, in part, to sustained and reform-resistant failures in U.S. K-12 education to produce higher general achievement in schooling and to reverse flat or downward trends in international mathematics and science comparisons [4]. Two recently-published reports by the National Academy of Education, for example, highlight teacher complaints about lack of personal agency or autonomy in teaching in high-stakes testing environments [5, 6]. While citing early-career teacher dropout rates and teachers' dissatisfaction and alienation in their profession, both reports highlight the need for more high-quality opportunities for professional growth than are currently available.

*Need 3: Teacher creativity is undervalued and underused.* A third need is related to the second, but has a lineage older than the current high-stakes policy structures. It also unlocks the potential contribution of Tablet PC-enabled innovation to national discourse on mathematical teacher professional development. The prominent role of traditional textbook or reform curriculum producers and curriculum standards and policies, the lack of effective tools for digital representation of mathematics, and the very limited time that teachers have outside of the classroom all act to crowd out the *creative potential* of teachers to generate content. As in the past, mathematics teachers are not expected to be content *producers*, but rather are content *conveyors*, following pre-defined curriculum in

**Table 1.** Tablet and screen video object design principles.

| | |
|---|---|
| • Video objects should require no more than 1-4 minutes to execute. | • Objects should map to specific content standards and expectations for the teacher's school or LEA. |
| • Objects should be self-contained, and open, execute and close in single clicks. Easy-on, easy-off, minimal searching by students, no disruption to classroom flow. | • The objects should form a trusted library that students can access autonomously both from within school firewalls and outside of school. |
| • When illustrating applets that require entering variable parameters by students, the teacher content should model the applet and show the student how to parameterize it, and provide a live link for their own experimentation. | • The library should grow over the course of a teacher's career, and represent content sharable within the teacher's professional networks. |
| | • Narration should be in the teacher's own voice where possible. |

preparation for accountability tests. At a time of unparalleled ascendency of user-generated content in society more broadly (as evidenced by phenomena such as YouTube), teachers are strangely left out. Mathematics teachers simply are not expected to be creative in producing content that maps to their students' needs or to their own teaching styles.

## 3. Solution Employed

In this project, twenty-one public school mathematics teachers from Los Angeles, Orange, and Ventura Counties have developed or adapted approximately one hundred short videos, two of which are discussed below. They are designed in compliance with the principles that appear in Table 1, principles at the heart of attempting to improve the usability of digital media in mathematics.

Tablet PC computers and screen video capture software are the project's foundational tools. The screen video capture allows teachers to narrate and record short videos on their Tablet PCs while using the Tablet PC-enabled and natural flowing form-factor of handwritten mathematical notation to enable them to replicate electronically board-like instruction. The purpose of the effort includes but also extends far beyond allowing teachers to replicate math lectures electronically and using the Tablet PCs for the notation that makes that possible. A larger and more sublime purpose is to draw teachers into the process of *reflective anticipation of the subtleties and nuances* students face with challenging mathematical material. Our data suggest that this occurs as a natural by-product of engaging teachers in the craft of video production. The practices of that craft include video take and re-take, mixing, matching and refining video sequences, and calibrating individual image against audience perception. The practices appear, based on numerous interviews, to engender more of the deep mathematical probing and sustained attention to content and cognition that have been cited as critical needs in professional development [7]. This pathway is a direct response to Needs 2 and 3, to deepen professional development opportunities, while helping teachers manage the high-stakes accountability requirements, and utilizing teacher creativity. The notion of teachers engaged in the disciplines of reflective anticipation through video production invokes a field of educational psychology called *microgenetic analysis*. Microgenetic analysis is an approach to cognitive science with a long history; its more prominent use began by the mid-1980s [e.g., 8]. The microgenetic approach to the study of cognitive process involves a high density of observations per unit of time—parallel, it turns out, to the exacting calibrations involved in video production. The approach has been critiqued as overly expensive and time-consuming as a research methodology. But in the day-to-day rhythm of professional development, reflection, and the creation and testing of interactive digital media, teachers may indeed be able to become applied scientists—microgenetic analysts, in other words—who draw on their experience to reverse engineer student cognitive pathways and design media to help students address subtle and knotty conceptual obstacles. We have coined the term "applied microgenetic analysts" to refer to teachers probing and building media to match cognition, not to invoke the kinds of theoretical inquiries commonly associated with microgenetic study of cognition, but instead to emulate the subtle and minute exploration of cognitive pathways, especially with digital media that tracks with those pathways. The teacher comments below reflect this experience.

A model of the overall path to sophistication in resource creation appears in Table 2, simple videos *de novo*, more complex videos *de novo,* and then revision and adaptation. Two examples illustrate the progression. Each has amateur edges, but they are authentic teacher constructions.

**Table 2:** Observed evolution of proficiencies in creating sharable content libraries.

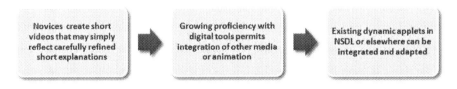

*Creating New Content.* Producing content from scratch is the straightforward process of teachers generating explanations or illustrations that they can use and reuse. Because content creation takes place outside of the live classroom setting, teachers can reflect more carefully and collaboratively on what they want to communicate. Teachers, like media producers more generally, are able to edit, reedit, and refine their presentations. Once they have developed the simple skills of producing short narrated videos, they transition to adding other audio or graphic or visualization tools to help build richness and interest in the material. The various objects that they have developed in the pilot activities include thirty to ninety second video clips explaining mathematical ideas, which often require nothing more than clearly walking through the idea structure. The teacher may elect to include in the set of questions those that are related to specific exercises. Questions may be related to statewide standards in the curriculum area (such as, "this question corresponds to state standard x, y, or z"). We also encourage teachers to develop multiple, narrated versions of playback solutions to problems, differing by level of elaboration of each step. So, for example, a student can retrieve playback of a specific problem and watch the teacher's solution unfold in real-time with an audio narration. A student who needs further help or clarification might retrieve a version of the solution that unpacks each step or starts at a more elementary level of explanation. Screenshots from the first example appear in Figure 1 (with the video available at http://erichamilton.net/alaskavideos). One is a simple review of sums and factors in quadratic factoring and involves a video screen capture of a handwritten explanation. The explanation is clear, has an easy-to-copy representational device (overlay the plus sign above a multiplication sign), is short, and can be replayed for the student. The other depicts simple polynomial multiplication, but again in a replayable and clear manner.

**Figure 1.** Two simple teacher-made videos.

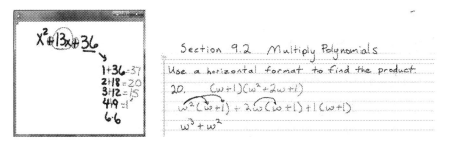

*Adapting Existing Content.* The mathematics education cyber-community has developed a growing cyber-sphere of content applets that teachers may confidently direct their students to use. But, as noted earlier, if a teacher can locate a valuable or compelling applet resource freely available online, it might not be useful with a whole class or lend itself to adaptation to full class lesson; and it might not be readily available when a student poses a question during a class discussion. It likely requires trial-and-error parameterizing and validation. A teacher may run a visualization prepared in advance and determine which parameters (e.g., values for variables, scale of axes, etc.) most effectively highlight an idea. That is, the teacher can fill in values, move sliders, use pallets, and actually carry out a visualization that resides in an existing digital repository. By capturing the teacher's running of the applet to video, students have easy access to the underlying mathematical idea and see how to perform the applet if they wish to parameterize it on their own. What is the advantage? First, such instruction on individual applets is time-intensive and distracting in classrooms. It just cannot happen frequently, nor is it realistic to expect otherwise. On the other hand, pretesting, authenticating, and storing the applet reference in the library can make it reliably and safely available to students. A second advantage goes directly to the use of annotation to furnish a new layer of explanation appropriate for extra assistance where desired. This further responds to Need 1, to render new and existing digital content more usable in live classroom settings.

*Conic section visualization.* In the free-throw applet [9] that 2 depicts, a short video of Justin Timberlake shooting free throws at the ESPY Awards is narrated by the teacher, who identifies salient features of the arc before shifting into a discussion of parabolic properties, demonstrating what effect each of the three (quadratic, linear, and constant) coefficients has on the arc. The video is less than one minute long. It maps sports and entertainment to parabola instruction, enabling a visualization of the factors influencing function behavior. It shows how to use parameter sliders on a visualization applet and invites students to manipulate the sliders themselves. The Tablet PC permits additional annotation layer over the applet that allows the teacher to insert written comments over the applet. In this case, the teacher "steps out" of the applet and provides explanatory information.

**Figure 2.** Conic section video first shows Justin Timberlake shooting a free throw, then an interactive applet modeling the free throw trajectory.

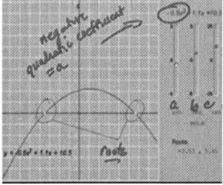

## 4. Evaluation

Teachers in this pilot work have shared an abundance of observations about the approach, through both informal and formal surveys and structured interviews. Each of these benefits corresponds to addressing the needs cited at the beginning of the paper, to make digital libraries more usable in classrooms, to enhance teacher professional development, and to leverage creativity. Teachers made these observations about the model:

- It promotes *technological fluency.* We are likely experiencing one of the first times in social history in which the generation being taught has greater overall fluency in the tools and media for knowledge archiving and expression than the generation that is teaching. One teacher wrote: "The library tool is a great addition to my teaching tool box. Not only does it allow me to be technologically more advanced and up-to-date with the latest innovations, it also makes me a much better critical thinker."

- The model promotes *intense pedagogical concentration.* The teachers anticipate the subtleties of potential misunderstandings. One teacher wrote in a formal survey, "(The professional development) definitely does exercise creativity because it makes me anticipate common mistakes students make and design media accordingly. It made me think like a student and allows me to use different visual effects to enhance the learning process." Another wrote, "Development of the templates for algebraic procedures has helped me focus on the degree to which students' spatial intelligence is as important as their math/logic intelligence." A third wrote "(Anticipating subtlety and nuance) . . . is one of the major advantages to using this library system. It has forced me to think of every little thing that students may have trouble with." Finally, one teacher wrote, "Designing the content is primarily based on anticipating the misconceptions."

- It creates *cumulative bodies of personalized, reusable, and modifiable pedagogical knowledge.* One teacher wrote, "It made me realize that using technology allows me to focus more on content rather than delivery because the library eliminates the need to worry about delivery on a daily basis. I create it once, and it's out there for students to refer to over and over again." Another wrote, "The library exercises my creativity in new ways by forcing me to perfect every single detail. I have this ability because I can erase and record the content. Also I can review my work and make changes if necessary."

## 5. Future Work

Two primary strands for future work appear most promising. On the application side, we are seeking to expand the number of teachers who build video content and can help refine the design principles for doing so. Additionally, project sites are in formation in several international venues in Asia, Africa, and Europe. On the research side, our interests involve understanding the evolution of teachers who create media in advance of the classes that they teach. This work is currently supported by IES. Additionally, the NSF National STEM Distributed Learning (NSDL) Program issued a grant in September 2010 to carry out targeted impact research on the project. As noted earlier, this work is connected to an underlying theory of personalized learning communities [10] and one avenue of research will entail applying that research. We will rely on and expand the construct of microgenetic analysis discussed earlier as one means to understand more fully teacher reflections and efforts to effectively map mathematical content tightly to student cognition through the creative use of digital media. Additionally, teachers as microgenetic analysts of student cognition lead to another major inquiry. Does assuming a more proactive role in media design to match student cognition alter the teacher's own cognitive processes? We hypothesize that engaging teachers in such analysis of learner cognition during development of digital media enhances their pedagogical flexibility, expertise, and sophistication. These research questions do not focus on the interface tools of Tablet PCs. Instead, Tablet PCs furnish a path to enable teachers to join the ranks of digital content producers in mathematics, and thus a new way to conceptualize professional development and the evolution of teachers as "connoisseurs" of learning.

## 6. Acknowledgments

The author gratefully acknowledges the support of the Institute for Education Sciences [1] and the National Science Foundation [2] in supporting this research.

## References

[1] Hamilton, E., and N. Harding. *IES Grant: Agent and Library Augmented Shared Knowledge Areas (ALASKA).* Institute for Education Sciences Award 305A080667, 2008.

[2] Hamilton, E. *PREDICATE Project: Targeted Research on Teacher Creativity at the Intersection of Content, Student Cognition, and Digital Media.* National Science Foundation award 1044478, 2010.

[3] National Science Foundation. *National Science Distributed Learning (NSDL) Program,* l.r. Program Announcement 10-545. http://www.nsf.gov/pubs/2010/nsf10545/nsf10545. htm?org=NSF, Editor, 2010.

[4] Sunderman, G., Kim, J., and Orfield, G. *NCLB meets school realities: Lessons from the field.* Corwin, 2005.

[5] Wilson, S. W., et al. *Teacher Quality: Education Policy White Paper of the National Academy of Education.* http://www.naeducation.org/Teacher_Quality_White_Paper.pdf, accessed Nov. 10, 2009.

[6] Kilpatrick, J., Quinn, H., Bass, H., Cobb, P., Daro, P., Gomez., L., et al. *Science and mathematics Education. Education Policy White Paper of the National Academy of Education.* http://www.naeducation.org/Science_and_Mathematics_Education_White_Paper.pdf, accessed Nov. 10, 2009.

[7] Ball, D. L. *Mathematical Proficiency for All Students: Toward a Strategic Research and Development Program in Mathematics Education.* RAND Corporation, 2003.

[8] Lawler, R. *Computer experience and cognitive development: A child's learning in a computer culture.* E. Horwood, 1985.

[9] Nelson, A. *Graphing Parabolas from the Justin Limberlake Free Throw. http://ghchs. edusims.com/alaska/videos/free-throw-to-graph.swf.__Granada Hills Charter High School,* 2009.

[10] Hamilton, E., and Jago, M. *Towards a Theory of Personalized Learning Communities,* in *Designs for Learning Environments of the Future.* M. Jacobson and R. Reimann (Eds.), Springer Press, 2010.

# A Method for Automating the Analysis of Tablet PC Ink-Based Student Work Collected Using DyKnow Vision

*Jared J. Hatfield*

*University of Louisville*

## 1. Abstract

Existing technologies and tools related to classroom management, such as DyKnow Vision, focus on the distribution and collection of student work. While this category of products focus on the generation of content, the management of student submitted work is still a manual process. Student work collected using this type of tool is generally confined to the application that was used to generate the work, requiring instructors to manually move data from one educational application to another. Instructor efficiency and enthusiasm for ink-based technologies could be improved with additional tools. This paper describes the development of a custom application to export and analyze the content of DyKnow files. Our application will reduce the amount of time required by an instructor to score digital ink-based student work submitted through DyKnow. After the initial step of reading the DyKnow file is overcome, the possibility for automating common administrative tasks is seemingly endless. A simple case for automation is reading in handwritten grades on a panel collected from students, and exporting student names and the assigned scores to a CSV file. More advanced application includes further automation of the grading process. These challenges are addressed and one potential solution has been developed.

## 2. Problem Statement and Context

One of the attractive features of an instructional setting that utilizes Tablet PCs is that student work can be completed and submitted electronically. A typical grading cycle outlined in Figure 1 includes a student submitting an assignment, the assignment being graded, and finally feedback being sent to the student, along with a numerical grade being recorded in the grade book. The specific segment in this workflow that can be optimized is the step between grading the student work and recording the numerical score in the grade book. In a pen and paper setting, the grade is recorded on the page and then transferred to the grade book. In an electronic setting, the grade can still be recorded on the panel, but the transferring to the grade book can be, at least partially, automated.

**Figure 1.** Standard workflow for grading student work.

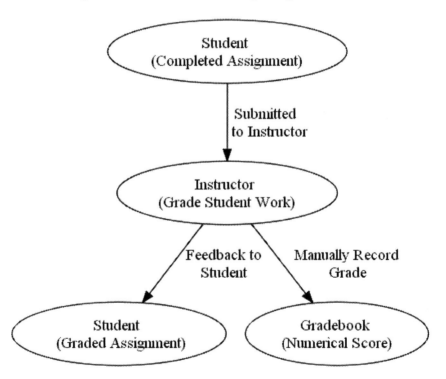

## 2.1 Technical Context for DPX Grader

DyKnow Vision [1] is a proprietary piece of software that utilizes a variety of Microsoft's technologies, including the InkCanvas for collecting pen-based input. The DyKnow file format consists of compressed XML that represents the serialized C# objects that are used by the DyKnow Vision application. Due to the descriptive nature of XML, it is possible to interpret the contents of a DyKnow file without access to the source code that was used to generate the file. The digital ink content of a DyKnow file is of particular interest because it represents a student's work or an instructor's score. This information can be algorithmically analyzed using Microsoft's ink recognition libraries. The ink recognition libraries allow for entire panels or specific regions of the panel to be analyzed and converted into text. Panels that are collected in a session also have the participants name and username embedded as an XML attribute for the panel. This metadata can be used to reduce the overhead when grading student work.

## 3. Solution Employed

DPX is an open source software project written in C# using Visual Studio 2008 and the .NET 3.5 framework. It consists of a collection of tools that are based around reading files created using DyKnow Vision. The current set of tools includes DPX Manager, DPX Preview, DPX Sorter, and DPX Grader, and descriptions of these tools can be found in Table 1. The tool that is capable of analyzing student work is known as DPX Grader.

**Table 1.** List of applications included as part of DPX.

| Application | Description |
| --- | --- |
| DPX Sorter | A tool for sorting panels in a DyKnow file by the collected participants username or full name |
| DPX Preview | A tool for opening DyKnow files and rendering the panels used primarily for determining the accuracy of DPX's rendering abilities by comparing panels to DyKnow |
| DPX Manager | Software for importing metadata from DyKnow files into a database for assigning credit to students based on best effort in the completion of a DyKnow panel [2] |
| DPX Grader | The next generation of DPX software that is able to algorithmically analyze and export handwritten grades |

## 3.1 Automated Extraction of Panel Information

To simplify the implementation of DPX Grader, the actual grading of student work occurs inside of DyKnow Vision, which is capable of editing DyKnow files. For the purposes of automation, a dedicated region of the panel can be set aside to record the grade. It is then possible to extract specific regions of ink from an InkCanvas containing the grade. For the example depicted in Figure 2, the top left corner is dedicated to a grade box as indicated by the shaded region. Additionally, the question is placed above the line while the student completes the question below the line. In the depicted panel, the student received five points for this problem. The number recorded can be algorithmically read using DPX Grader and then converted into a numeric representation. This approach is not novel, but mirrors the practice that has previously existed using pen and paper.

**Figure 2.** Completed student work.

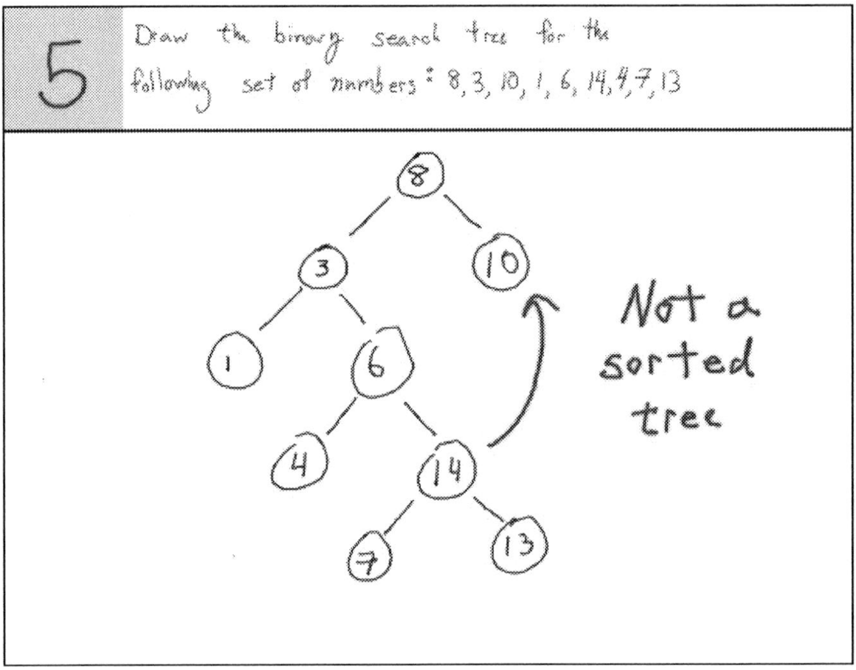

DPX Grader is divided into a three-step process as seen in Figure 3. The first step is opening the DyKnow file that is to be processed. The second step is choosing the specific region of the panel that is to be processed and converted to text. In this application a square of varying sizes can be placed in any of the four corners. Once the desired region has been selected, which can be set to match a region that was shaded on the original panel, the group of panels is ready to be processed. The entire set of panels can then be processed and the results shown in table form (step three).

**Figure 3.** The interface for DPX Grader.

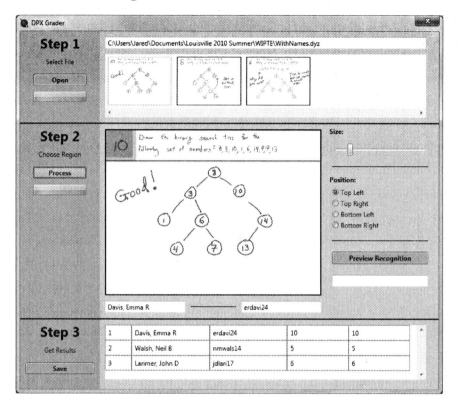

The output from DPX Grader, as shown in Table 2, displays the information that was contained within the processed DyKnow file. If the set of panels was collected in session, the participant's full name and username are included; otherwise the fields are left blank. The region of the panel that was recognized is converted into text; then, using a parsing algorithm, is converted to a numeric representation if possible. The output is exported as CSV file, which can be opened by standard software such as Excel.

Table 2. The results from the processing of a DyKnow file using DPX Grader.

| Panel Number | Participant Full Name | Participant Username | Recognized Text | Numeric Text |
|---|---|---|---|---|
| 1 | Davis, Emma R | erdavi24 | 10 | 10 |
| 2 | Walsh, Neil B | nmwals14 | 5 | 5 |
| 3 | Larimer, John D | jdlari17 | 6 | 6 |

## 4. Evaluation

DPX Grader is still in the early stages of development and is designed to serve as a reference for what is possible when software is created to address the common tasks that educators are required to perform. The biggest obstacle is the amount of data and processing time required to perform this type of task. Even with a modern computer, the task of manipulating this type of content and performing recognition is very computationally expensive. The task of loading, rendering, and analyzing ink-based content is a time-consuming process when performed on such a large scale. To date the system has been tested successfully with a class enrolling one hundred students. As the data set grows to larger sizes, the amount of time required to process the data increases linearly. This task lends itself to parallel processing and is accelerated on computers with multiple cores.

### 4.1 Accuracy of Automated Analysis

The handwriting recognition libraries used are Microsoft's, and the accuracy of the recognition is dependent on external factors such as the individual's handwriting. Therefore, the automated analysis of ink-based content is not without some risk. Problems can arise with the inaccurate recognition of content on the panels. Modern handwriting recognition techniques, while accurate, are not perfect. The task of recognizing recorded grades is particularly difficult because a grade that is recorded consists only of a few numbers. While it is technically possible to perform ink recognition on an entire panel, this is very time-consuming, and the output is typically less than accurate or not useful. The approach used by DPX Grader is to let the user specify a small region on the panel and take the subset of pen strokes that fall inside that region. This information is specified by the application, but could be algorithmically computed using an element embedded on the panel itself, such as an Answer Box.

### 4.2 Benefit to Instructor

While DyKnow provides a robust software solution for classroom presentation and is designed to foster student engagement, the interpretation of student submitted work lies well outside of this focus area. By implementing a solution that focuses on using existing technologies to automate the process of extracting student names and interpreting handwritten grades, the door is opened for extensive automation. The goal is not to replace the instructor or the process of providing feedback to students, but to reduce the "manual" labor of processing electronically submitted work. The creation of a tool that is easy to use, yet flexible enough to be used in a wide variety of situations, attempts to reduce the negative aspects of moving to a paperless classroom.

# 5. Future Work

## 5.1 Complete DyKnow File Read/Write Capability

The file specification for DyKnow Vision is not freely available due to the methods employed by DyKnow in the generation of files. Using Microsoft's C# XML deserialization methods, it is possible to map components of the XML document directly into memory. The difficulty in this task is that XML automatically collapses those unused parts of the specification. This requires that DyKnow files be generated that utilize all of the various components of the DyKnow file specification. Regression test and specialized software have been generated to test the accuracy of file deserialization and successive serialization, but without assistance from DyKnow, it would be impossible to ensure compatibility across all variations of DyKnow files.

The current implementation of the DPX panel rendering engine is not capable of displaying all the components that can be included on a panel. The most glaring omission is text-based content that can be written on the panel or placed inside of a text box. Additionally, the inclusion of panel history complicates the process of rendering ink-based content that has been moved or resized. However, the ink-based content can be correctly interpreted by removing a panel's history from within DyKnow Vision. While it was possible to construct a method to test the accuracy of file deserialization, the process of checking panel rendering accuracy is significantly more difficult.

## 5.2 Ability to Read other File Types

The ability to read in other types of files is very important for this category of tool. Classroom Presenter [3] is an obvious next choice for files that could be processed using this tool. While Classroom Presenter is open source, the approach used in the storage of files generated by Classroom Presenter makes reading in files by third party applications very difficult. The software uses binary serialization on top of older, Windows Forms-based components. While it is not impossible, the amount of work required to read in this type of file is much greater than reading in DyKnow files, even with the source code for Classroom Presenter available.

## 5.3 Automated Analysis of Student Responses

DyKnow provides an Answer Box element that can be added to a panel that provides a dedicated region that is intended to contain an answer. While DyKnow does not take advantage of this distinction, it could be used to isolate the region of ink for the purposes of handwriting recognition. Expanding on the abilities of DPX Grader, it is possible to automate the analysis of the student responses so they can be compared to the correct answers. The limitations of handwriting recognition will require an intelligent algorithm that analyzes the list of valid answers and the recognized text, including alternatives, to compute a confidence level. This type of tool would provide a streamlined and automated method for grading student work.

## 6. Additional Resources

DPX-Tools is a suite of open source applications developed by Jared Hatfield and is licensed under a GNU General Public License v3. The source code and installation package is available at the project's page on Google Code: http://code. google.com/p/dyknow-panel-extractor/.

## References

[1] http://www.dyknow.com. DyKnow company Web site.

[2] Hatfield, J. J., Hieb, J. L., and Lewis, J. E. Using Retrieved Panels from DyKnow for Large Classes. *The Impact of Tablet PCs and Pen-Based Technology on Education.* Purdue University Press, 2009.

[3] http://classroompresenter.cs.washington.edu/. Classroom Presenter Web site.

# The Note-Taker: A Tablet PC-based Device that Helps Students Take and Review Classroom Notes

*David S. Hayden, Liqing Zhou, and John A. Black Jr.*

*Arizona State University*

## 1. Abstract

The act of note-taking is crucially important to learning in secondary and post-secondary classrooms. It helps students to stay focused on the instruction, forces them to cognitively process what is being presented, and helps them to better retain what has been taught, even if they never subsequently refer to their notes. This paper describes ongoing research and development of a device (called the Note-Taker) that a student can take to class to assist in the process of taking notes. It describes the principles that have guided the development of the Note-Taker prototype, and presents the results of preliminary usability studies that have been conducted with post-secondary students who have visual disabilities.

## 2. Problem Statement and Context

### 2.1 Note-taking as a Recording Process

Note-taking is widely regarded as being crucially important to learning in secondary and post-secondary classrooms. However, not all researchers view the note-taking process in the same way. One view is that it is a process of *recording* the information presented in the classroom, in a form that can be archived and later reviewed. Based on that view, several high-technology alternatives to individual classroom note-taking have been proposed, such as digital whiteboards and lecture recording systems.

Digital whiteboards (sometimes called interactive whiteboards) can be used to automatically transfer writing on a whiteboard into a digital representation, which can be stored (and later viewed) on a desktop or laptop computer. When used in this manner, digital whiteboards can be viewed as a component of a *recording* device. The LiveBoard [5] running the Tivoli [9] application was the first proposed digital whiteboard, followed by other solutions in both research and commercial settings [8, 12]. Some of these later approaches, such as Mimeo [8], employ a device that can be attached to a conventional whiteboard, to allow its use as a digital whiteboard. However, such a device is not practical for general classroom use because it supports only a single whiteboard of a rather limited size.

An alternative classroom recording approach is to record the entire lecture as a video, with accompanying audio. Apreso Classroom [2] and AutoAuditorium [3] offer automatic recording of lectures through the use of semi-permanent camera setups. A recording system described in [13] captures video of overhead presentations, and then summarizes that video, using key frames. Another system called PhotoNote [7] (which is designed to assist students with vision or hearing impairments) employs two camcorders and one still-image camera. One camcorder is aimed at the lecturer, and the other is aimed at a sign language interpreter. Meanwhile the still-image camera takes a high resolution (eight megapixel) photo every three seconds. All three of these image streams are synchronized, recorded, and made available for the student after the class.

### 2.2 Note-taking as an Assimilative Process

An alternative view of note-taking is that it is a cognitive assimilation process. While taking notes, the student is engaged mentally to (1) understand what is being said; (2) decide what is new, and what is already known; and (3) record what is necessary for that student to recall what was taught. This view of note-taking is supported by the finding that note-taking helps students retain important information, even if they do not review their notes after class [6]. Students who take notes also perform better on far-transfer tasks such as problem solving, which is central to science, engineering, and mathematics [11]. In general, note-taking promotes a deeper level of understanding, because an assimilative process is engaged [4, 10]. The problem with relying on a high-technology recording system (as a substitute for classroom note-taking) is that it leaves the student out of the process.

The student (1) has no control over the recording system during the lecture; (2) is dependent upon someone else to process and deliver the recorded information; and (3) is not able to view and listen to the recording until *after* the lecture. Some would argue that recording lectures may discourage students from class participation—or even class attendance.

### 2.3 The Challenges Faced by Students with Visual Disabilities

Students with visual disabilities often require assistive technologies to view their notes, or to view material presented at the front of a classroom. The most commonly used assistive device is a handheld or head-mounted monocular. Higher-tech alternatives include manually-operated swivel cameras that output to an external display, or head-mounted camera display systems. Each of these provide magnification for far-sight tasks (such as viewing a whiteboard) or for near-sight tasks (such as viewing or taking notes), but none facilitate rapid transitions between the two. This puts students with visual disabilities at a significant disadvantage in the classroom because note-taking involves rapid shifts in focus between a distant board and the student's notes.

The Americans with Disabilities Act [1] mandates the availability of human note-takers who can provide students with copies of their notes. As with lecture recording systems, the problem with this approach is that the student loses the benefits of classroom note-taking and might not be as likely to ask questions and initiate discussions during the class presentation. Additionally, the notes may not account for the student's preferred style or existing knowledge.

## 3. Solution Employed

### 3.1 Principles to Guide the Development of a Note-Taker Device

We initially set out to design a solution that allows students with visual disabilities to take notes in class. Such a solution must provide access to all relevant aspects of a classroom presentation, facilitate real-time note-taking, and provide effective mechanisms for later review. As we proceeded with the development of the Note-Taker, we realized that it might be appealing to all students.

The following principles guided the development of the Note-Taker:

(1) It should be portable and self-contained. It should not force the user to be dependent on other students, the lecturer, the technical staff, or a classroom infrastructure.

(2) It should not be disruptive to student interactions with peers or with the lecturer.

(3) It should provide real-time access to all relevant aspects of the classroom presentation and should facilitate both handwritten and typed notes.

(4) It should be practical for a student (i.e., it should fit into a backpack and should be reasonably priced).

## 3.2 The Development of Note-Taker 2.0

Based on our development and evaluation of an early proof-of-concept Note-Taker (built with an off-the-shelf camcorder, pan/tilt device, and Tablet PC) the National Science Foundation provided funding to develop a portable note-taking device that we call Note-Taker 2.0. This device consists of a Tablet PC, a custom-designed pan/tilt/zoom (PTZ) camera prototype (shown in Figure 1), and software that provides a special split-screen interface for simultaneously viewing the front of the classroom and taking handwritten or typed notes. The camera is a USB peripheral that employs a Sony industrial video camera with 36x zoom, two servo motors, and a battery that supports more than five hours of use. Figure 2 shows the complete Note-Taker setup. A view of a whiteboard at the front of the classroom is seen in the top half of the Tablet PC display, and the digital notepad for taking handwritten notes is seen at the bottom.

**Figure 1.** The pan/tilt/zoom camera.

**Figure 2.** The Note-Taker 2.0 prototype.

### 3.3 Note-Taker 2.0 Features

The student can take notes while simultaneously viewing live video with a split-screen interface. This interface allows for rapid transitions between taking notes and viewing presentation material, and can provide close-up views of the board, making it suitable for students with visual disabilities.

There are three methods to control the camera. The first method allows the student to center the camera on any feature that is visible within the video window (such as the professor) by simply tapping that feature. The camera quickly centers on that feature, which then becomes the focal point for subsequent zooms.

Alternatively, the user can touch any feature in the image and drag their finger to another location within the window. The camera will keep the feature under the user's finger by panning and tilting accordingly. Third, students can use multi-touch pinch and un-pinch gestures to zoom out or zoom in the camera, respectively.

Lecturers will sometimes step in front of what they have previously written on the board while students are trying to copy it. To deal with this problem the Note-Taker extracts one video frame per second and retains that frame for ten seconds. If the instructor occludes the board, the student can "look back" through these frames to find one that was captured before the board content was occluded. When ready, the student can then resume with the live video.

With multiple classes (each with two to three sessions per week) a student can rapidly accumulate a huge amount of files. The Note-Taker software provides structure by managing recorded notes, video, audio, and screenshots) based on "note-taking sessions" that are sorted by class and date.

## 4. Evaluation

Early usability testing of the Note-Taker 2.0 PTZ camera is being conducted under controlled classroom conditions. In recruiting participants, preference has been given to students who have visual disabilities. The participants are first shown how to use both the tapping method and the dragging method for aiming the camera. Then they are shown how to use pinching and un-pinching motions to control zoom. Finally they are asked to perform the following five camera control tasks, which are typical of what they might need to do in a classroom setting.

> Task 1 employs a Snellen eye chart as a visual stimulus and is designed to motivate the participants to progressively zoom in the camera as they go down the chart, line by line.

> Task 2 presents three long equations on a whiteboard. This task is designed to trade off increasing zoom against decreasing field of view.

> Task 3 presents eleven unusual words written on a whiteboard. Participants are asked to repeatedly find and read aloud a word to which an investigator points.

> Task 4 presents a periodic table of elements. Participants are asked to first search the table for a designated element, and then to read its atomic weight, which requires extreme zoom.

Task 5 presents nine phrases that run the width of a white board. This task is designed to cause the participants to use the panning function of the camera to progressively scan the phrases from left to right, while reading them aloud.

## 5. Results

Three participants were asked to perform these five tasks, with corrected visual acuity ranging from 20/30 to 20/800 in their best eye. At the conclusion of each of the five tasks, the participants were asked to express their agreement or disagreement with four or five statements, to which they were asked to respond on a Likert scale from 1 to 7, where 1 means "Strongly disagree" and 7 means "Strongly agree." The results are shown in Table 1. (The results for the student with the most severe visual disability (i.e. 20/800) are shown in **bold**.)

**Table 1.** Usability testing results: Likert scores—Strongly disagree = 1, Strongly agree = 7

| | |
|---|---|
| **Task 1** | |
| The camera allows you to read the letters on the eye chart more easily | 6,6,**7** |
| The tapping method for aiming the camera is useful for this task | 6,6,**7** |
| The touch-and-drag method for aiming the camera is useful for this task | 4,5,**7** |
| You have to zoom in and zoom out a lot to do this task | 6,7,**7** |
| **Task 2** | |
| The camera has a wide enough field of view that you could see the entire equation | **6,7,7** |
| The tapping method for aiming the camera is useful for this task | 1,1,**7** |
| The touch-and-drag method for aiming the camera is useful for this task | 1,1,**3** |
| You have to zoom in and zoom out a lot to do this task | 1,1,**2** |
| You have to move the camera a lot to see the entire equation | 1,1,**5** |
| **Task 3** | |
| You are able to easily move to and read each new word | 4,5,**6** |
| The tapping method for aiming the camera is useful for this task | **5**,7,7 |
| The touch-and-drag method for aiming the camera is useful for this task | **5**,7,7 |
| You have to zoom in and zoom out a lot to do this task | 2,4,**7** |
| **Task 4** | |
| You are able to easily move to and read the molecular weight of each element | 1,3,**6** |
| The tapping method for aiming the camera is useful for this task | **5**,6,6 |
| The touch-and-drag method for aiming the camera is useful for this task | 3,6,**7** |
| You have to zoom in and zoom out a lot to do this task | **7,7,7** |
| **Task 5** | |
| You are able to easily move to and read each new phrase | 6,7,**7** |
| The tapping method for aiming the camera is useful for this task | 1,6,**7** |
| The touch-and-drag method for aiming the camera is useful for this task | **4**,6,7 |
| You have to zoom in and zoom out a lot to do this task | 1,1,**2** |
| **Overall Evaluation** | |
| Overall, this camera is easy to use | 3,6,**6** |
| Overall, the tapping method for aiming the camera is easy to use | 4,5,**6** |
| Overall, the touch-and-drag method for aiming the camera is easy to use | 4,5,**7** |
| Overall, the pinching method for zooming in and zooming out is easy to use | 1,1,**6** |
| You would like to use this camera in your classrooms | **7,7,7** |

In general, while the participants liked the methods for controlling the aim and the zoom level of the camera, they felt that the implementation should be faster and more precise. Despite these problems, all of the participants agreed with the statement that they would like to use the camera in their classrooms.

## 6. Future Work

Based on feedback from our ongoing usability testing, improvements are being developed for incorporation into the next generation Note-Taker 3.0 device. Figure 3 shows two views of our proposed Note-Taker 3.0 PTZ camera. The left-hand image shows what the PTZ camera unit would look like when in use, and right-hand image shows what the camera unit would look like when closed for transport. The whole mechanism can then be slipped into a protective case, for transport in the student's backpack.

**Figure 3.** The Note-Taker 3.0 PTZ Camera.

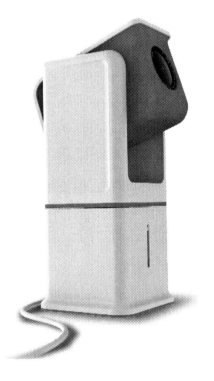 

In addition to this new camera, the following features are planned for Note-Taker 3.0.

1. A means for rapidly capturing video frames and inserting them into the notes, to reduce the need for copying complicated diagrams or equations.

2. Additional file management features, including an intelligent file management system that stores files created during classroom sessions, based on time of day and the calendar date.

3. Provisions for archiving Note-Taker files onto external media, such as DVDs.

4. A comprehensive review facility that allows students to view and search synchronized audio, video, screenshots, and notes.

5. A motion tracking feature that allows the Note-Taker camera to follow the professor, while allowing the student to take manual control of the camera as necessary.

## 7. Acknowledgments

This material is based in part upon work supported by the National Science Foundation under grant number IIS-0931278. Any opinions, findings, and conclusions or recommendations expressed in this material are those of the author(s) and do not necessarily reflect the views of the National Science Foundation.

## References

[1] ada.gov, Americans with Disabilities Act, Sec. 12189. Examinations and Courses. [Section 208]. http://www.ada.gov/pubs/ada.htm, 1990.

[2] Apreso. http://www.apreso.com/ac_product_overview.asp.

[3] Autoauditorium. http://www.autoauditorium.com/.

[4] Einstein, G. O., and Others, A. Note-Taking, Individual Differences, and Memory for Lecture Information. *Journal of Educational Psychology*, 77 (1985) 522-532.

[5] Elrod, S., Bruce, R., Gold, R., Goldberg, D., Halasz, F., Janssen, W., Lee, D., Mccall, K., Pedersen, E., Pier, K., Tang, J., and Welch, B. Liveboard: a large interactive display supporting group meetings, presentations, and remote collaboration. In *Proceedings of the SIGCHI conference on Human factors in computing systems*. Monterey, California, 1992, 599-607.

[6] Hartley, J., and Davies, I.K. Note-taking: A critical review. *Innovations in Education and Teaching International*, 15 (1978) 207.

[7] Hughes, G., and Robinson, P. Photonote evaluation: aiding students with disabilities in a lecture environment. In *Proceedings of the 9th international ACM SIGACCESS conference on Computers and accessibility*, 2007, 99-106.

[8] Mimeo. *Interactive whiteboard, virtual whiteboard, whiteboards, mimio.* http://www.mimio.com/.

[9] Minneman, S., Harrison, S., Janssen, B., Kurtenbach, G., Moran, T., Smith, I., and Van Melle, B. A confederation of tools for capturing and accessing collaborative activity. *Proceedings of the third ACM international conference on Multimedia*, San Francisco, California, 1995, 523-534.

[10] Peper, R. J., and Mayer, R. E. Note Taking as a Generative Activity. *Journal of Educational Psychology, 70.4* (1978) 514-522

[11] Peper, R. J., and Mayer, R. E. Generative Effects of Note-Taking during Science Lectures. *Journal of Educational Psychology, 78* (1986) 34-38.

[12] Smart Technologies. *The SMART Board.* http://smarttech.com/.

[13] Weller, G. *An Automatic Lecture Note Taker.* Report—BSCS. Department of Computer Science, University of Sheffield, 2004.

# A Digital Ink and Computer Algebra System Mashup to Enhance Classroom Learning

*Jeffrey L. Hieb*

*University of Louisville*

## 1. Abstract

There are obvious benefits to using digital ink and Tablet PCs in mathematics classes. But in a 1:1 Tablet PC deployment the use of digital ink should not pre-empt or prevent the use of other software to enhance classroom learning even further. The Computer Algebra System (CAS) Maple offers extensive computation capabilities, which could significantly enhance classroom learning if integrated well. This paper presents a method for presenting students with a pen-friendly GUI to Maple computation capabilities relevant to a specific in-class activity. Three of these activities were developed and tested in a Linear Algebra class taught in the spring semester of 2010. Technical difficulties experienced during deployment limited the impact of the developed activities; however, a statistically significant improvement on the average of one exam was observed.

## 2. Problem Statement and Context

Tablet PC environments that are 1:1 offer considerable opportunities for enhancing classroom learning. For example, in mathematics courses formulas and mathematical symbols are not easy to type, so digital ink is very attractive to both students and instructors. Sharing, capture, and replay of an instructor's ink can aid student learning. However, computational software or simulation software could also be used by students on their Tablet PCs during class as part of a designed activity. For example, if students are looking at an application of integration by attempting to solve a "real world problem," digital ink is a good medium for sketching and setting up the problem, but having a Computer Algebra System (CAS) like Maple evaluate the integral would make completing the exercise more efficient. The computation engine can handle the integration, no matter how messy, and serve up an answer quickly. Students can then interpret results, writing out a final solution in digital ink, and possibly have time to make corrections if needed. The problem with implementing this is that interacting with other software applications is usually not readily done with a pen. If the Tablet PC is in slate mode and a student is taking notes in some inking application, they can either attempt to use the pen, or switch out of slate mode to access the keyboard and track pad. Neither of these is highly desirable since this focuses the students' attention away from the learning activity and into "computer operator mode." What is needed is a way to combine both the digital ink and a CAS so that students can use specific computational capabilities relevant to a given activity. It is equally important that students be able to access these computational abilities easily and naturally using only the pen. The problem then is how to create a "mashup" of a CAS (Maple in this case) and a CLS (DyKnow in this case).

Some previous work in this area has been conducted by Joshua Holden [1]. Holden has used MapleNet to embed Maple graphs and plots into DyKnow as Web pages. These are embedded as applets so some limited interactivity and animation are possible, but full use of the Maple command line is not provided, nor can parameters or functions be changed. The solution described in Section 3 is a DyKnow Maple mashup that allows students to access targeted Maple functionality inside a DyKnow panel using only their pen. The class for which the solution was investigated is Linear Algebra for Engineers, taught by the author at the J. B. Speed School of Engineering.

## 3. Solution Employed

The solution employed was to develop Maple documents tailored specifically for a class activity. These documents used Maple's GUI components so they can be operated using a Tablet PC pen. The documents were then placed in the directory structure of MapleNet. MapleNet is a Servlet, most often used with Tomcat, which makes Maple documents accessible through a browser. Finally the Web page for the developed Maple document, served up by MapleNet, is embedded into a DyKnow Panel that is part of the prepared notes for a class meeting. The following sections trace this process for a specific document, one designed to have students use elementary row operations on an augmented matrix to solve a system of equations.

### 3.1 Learning Activity: Elementary Row Operations and Gaussian Elimination

This activity follows a short introduction to elementary row operations, row echelon form, elementary row operations, and back substitution. For the activity, students are to write the system of equations corresponding to a given augmented matrix, then put the matrix in row echelon form using Gaussian elimination, and finally find the solution using back substitution. Choosing the correct elementary row operations requires some analysis and understanding of the Gaussian elimination, but actually computing the subsequent matrix is a very rote and tedious process in which the likelihood for error is high (especially when many operations are performed). The goal is to embed a Maple document that allows the user to choose row operations but does the row operation computation and displays the resulting matrix.

### 3.2 Maple Document

Figure 1 shows the Maple document created for this exercise. Each of the three elementary row operations are available using drop-down lists and buttons, both of which can be operated with the pen. The starting matrix is algorithmically generated using a random number generator. The reset button will clear the memory and generate a new matrix. Row operation buttons use the values in the appropriate dropdown boxes to perform the indicated row operation, store the result, and update the display to the new matrix. When students get the matrix into row echelon form, the text "ROW ECHELON FORM" is displayed below the matrix. Figure 1 shows the initial document when loaded and after row operations have been used to put the matrix in row echelon form.

### 3.3 Serving Up the Document through the Internet: MapleNet

MapleNet, with some limitations on command line access, can serve up a Maple document as a single Web page. For this evaluation, Tomcat was used as the Web server, and MapleNet runs behind Tomcat. Setup and configuration of MapleNet are not trivial, and it is beyond the scope of this paper to discuss in detail. Simply put, once MapleNet is running correctly, you can place a Maple document in a directory under /usr/local/tomcat/webapps/maplenet and then access the document using a browser and the identifying URL. Requirements on the client side are to have the most recent version of the Java Runtime Environment installed and a Java-compatible browser.

**Figure 1.** Elimination activity Maple document, (a) starting and (b) row echelon forms.

**(a)**

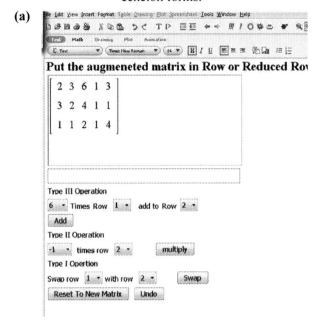

**(b)**

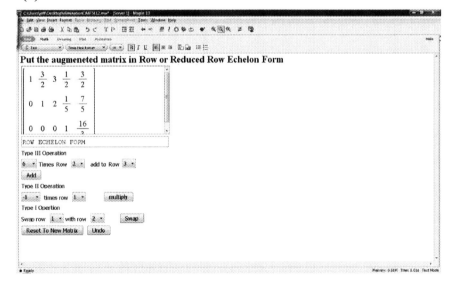

## 3.4 Embedding in DyKnow

DyKnow is a CLS where students and instructors use a shared whitespace during class (session). DyKnow notebooks are similar to PowerPoint presentations, and DyKnow panels are similar to PowerPoint slides. Prior to class, instructors can create a set of prepared notes, which can then be used in the session. In addition to text and pictures, live Web pages can be embedded into DyKnow Panels. These Web pages can take up either the whole panel or half a panel. To make both the document and inking available, a split screen embedded page was used. The Maple document was embedded on the left half of the screen. The right half left work space for the student to write the system of equations and space to solve the system once it is in row echelon form (or reduced row echelon form). Figure 2 shows a panel with the Maple Document embedded in the left half of the screen.

**Figure 2.** DyKnow panel with embedded Maple.

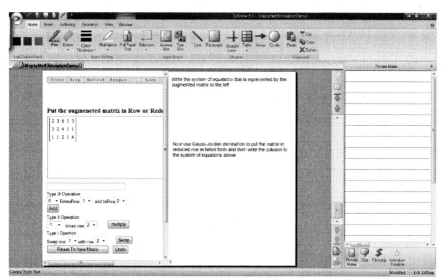

## 3.5 During Class

Once embedded into a DyKnow panel, the developed Maple document is ready to be used during a class activity. In this class activity the instructor presents elementary row operations, Gaussian elimination, and row echelon form in a traditional lecture format, and does some hand elementary row operations to demonstrate the elimination technique. At this point the DyKnow panel with the embedded Maple is brought into the session. First the instructor works the problem in private ink (which is not transmitted to students' Tablet PCs) and demonstrates how GUI components work to the students. At the same time the instructor is reinforcing the Gaussian elimination process. Since the Matrix is auto generated, each student has a different matrix in their panel on DyKnow, so students cannot just copy the instructor's solution. Next, time is given for students to work the problem, and they can even talk quietly about the activity since each has their own matrix to solve. It is important to note that, in order for the students to use the buttons, the moderator must enable browsing for the students, an option set in the DyKnow console.

## 4. Evaluation

In the spring semester of 2010, two sections of Linear Algebra for Engineers were taught by the author, and a comparison of student grades was done to examine the impact of the DyKnow Maple mashup on the experimental group. Twenty-nine students were enrolled in section one and twenty-seven students in section two. Section one served as the control group and section two the experimental group, with three DyKnow Maple mashup activities incorporated into the class. Development time was limited so only three activities were developed, and these roughly corresponded to the first half of the class. The activity described in Section 3 was one of the activities. A graphical exploration of the solution space of different systems of equations was another activity. The last activity was exploration of an application of linear transformations to two dimensional graphics.

Unexpected technical challenges arose when these were used in class, and this likely limited the effectiveness of the developed approach. During development and testing of modules, two Tablet PCs were used, the instructor's Fujitsu 5150 and an HP TC4400. The embedded Maple documents worked as expected on both the instructor's computer and a "test" student computer. The first "mashup," graphical exploration of the solution space of systems of linear equations, was used the second week of class. A number of students experienced difficulties getting the Maple document to operate correctly. In some cases the GUI components did not operate the document, in other cases the graphical component did not render at all, and in some other cases the entire page failed to load. For other students the embedded Maple worksheet worked fine. These problems persisted into the second and third times the embedded Maple was used, though to a less extent. The exact problem in all cases was never resolved, but contributing factors that were determined were settings in Internet Explorer and not having an up-to-date Java Runtime Environment. Some tutorials were quickly built to help students alleviate these issues, but students appeared to need more technical help than could be provided. However, those who did not experience technical difficulties were able to use the DyKnow Maple mashup activity as intended.

A comparison of the average on each exam shows that the experimental and the control group scored nearly equally well on the first exam, but on subsequent exams, the experimental group's average on each exam was higher. A more detailed analysis using a standard two sample T-Test assuming unequal variances found a significant statistical difference only on the fourth exam. The last DyKnow Maple mashup activity was completed just before the third exam. This suggests that the Maple DyKnow mashup activities might have impacted students' exam scores, either by providing a reinforcement of basic concepts (Activity 1 and 2) or by motivating interest though an interactive demonstration of an application (Activity 3). This is not strong evidence of a positive impact, and the technical difficulties experienced during use of the DyKnow Maple mashups may have prevented them from having a more positive effect.

Observation during the class indicated that students were receptive to this kind of interactive content and were excited when they were able to accomplish the activity when not impaired by technical challenges. A surprising observation was that several students conducted "what if" experiments by just entering numbers into the GUI for the linear transformation activity. Because the GUI was easy to use with their pen, "trying" things was easier. That the activity was unique to them and, in the case of the linear transformation activity, lack a specific correct answer seemed to free students from their common approach of "just tell me what the answer is."

**Table 1.** Two sample T-Test analysis of exams scores for the control and experimental group, (Control: n = 29, Experimental: n = 27).

| | Exam 1 | | Exam 2 | | Exam 3 | | Exam 4 | | Exam 5 | |
|---|---|---|---|---|---|---|---|---|---|---|
| | Ctrl. | Exper. | Ctrl. | Exper. | Ctrl. | Exper. | Ctrl. | Exper. | Ctrl. | Exper. |
| Mean | 0.813 | 0.806 | 0.645 | 0.698 | 0.615 | 0.696 | 0.745 | 0.836 | 0.816 | 0.847 |
| Std. Dev | 0.119 | 0.138 | 0.160 | 0.142 | 0.190 | 0.216 | 0.168 | 0.161 | 0.120 | 0.126 |
| t-statistics | 0.199832 | | -1.30765 | | -1.48525 | | -2.07391 | | -0.935342 | |
| P-value | 0.842399 | | 0.196543 | | 0.143532 | | 0.0428746 | | 0.353833 | |

## 5. Future Work

There are several important directions for future work related to this project. Clearly, the first is to address the technical difficulties experienced when evaluating the DyKnow Maple mashup. This may be challenging in a 1:1 environment where students own their own Tablet PCs, but a test DyKnow Maple mashup that exercises all the (GUI) functionality that any DyKnow Maple mashup could identify technical difficulties before they are experienced during an activity. There are other possible deployment environments that could be considered as well, such as Applets. Additional studies on the impact of this approach on student learning are needed as well, and these can be done while investigating and developing additional specific in-class activities for linear algebra or other engineering mathematics classes. If the technical interference is removed, this approach could be a very effective way to make class more active and motivate student learning. Leveraging the combination of ink with computational software in a classroom is still very new, but the solution presented here shows there are many possibilities. In fact, a case can easily be made that other disciplines, using different software, could benefit from other types of "mashups." Exploring this approach in other disciplines, developing common pedagogical and technological approaches, and quantifying the benefits for student learning are significant directions for future research.

## 6. Acknowledgments

This research was funded by a Scholarship of Teach and Learning Grant (SOTL) from the University of Louisville.

## References

[1] Holden, J., Sexton, S., and Williams, J. Math in Your Hands: Integrating the use of Maple with Collaborative use of Wireless Tablet PCs. In *The Impact of Tablet PCs and Pen-based Technology on Education*. D. Berque, L. Konkle, and R. Reed (Eds.). Purdue Uiversity Press, 2009, 57-64.

# Open Policy for Wireless Computers in Classrooms: What Makes it a Good or a Bad Idea?

*Zdeslav Hrepic and Kimberly Shaw*

*Columbus State University*

## 1. Abstract

Increasingly, studies and media articles have been looking into possible adverse effects of open policies for using wireless ready computers in classrooms. Tablet PCs, as indicated by some of those authors, are under suspicion more than laptops because they make it harder for the instructor to determine whether they are used productively or for off-the-task purposes. In this study students were invited to voluntarily bring their personal wireless computers to introductory physics classes in order to utilize them with DyKnow software. We compare performance of students who consistently used computers in classroom with those who did so less frequently or not at all. We also gauge how student attitudes and recommendations related to DyKnow software and Tablet PCs vary by type of computer that was available to them in this course.

## 2. Problem Statement and Context

A recent article in *The Washington Post* titled "More colleges, professors shutting down laptops and other digital distractions" [6] cites a number of references that question the educational benefits of allowing students to use wireless ready computers in classrooms. Ideally mobile computers would be used to take notes and search for relevant information. If misused, however, they may be a distraction for the user, as well as for students in vicinity and for the instructor. Fried [4] showed that students who use wireless laptops in classes may be frequently distracted from the task at hand, which negatively reflects on their performance. Barak at al [1] found that if wireless laptops are employed only when the instructor requires the students to do so, they may productively facilitate active learning. Otherwise, they may be used for Web surfing and e-mail messaging. Mortkowitz [6] contends Tablet PCs or devices like the iPad will only make it harder for students to pay attention in class. Because they can be used to read textbooks, it might be more difficult for professors to determine which students are off task and which are studying [6]. Sisson [7], however, very successfully deployed Tablet PCs to facilitate collaborative problem solving and saw considerable test score increase as well as significantly improved retention (>2 standard deviations) in her first semester algebra-based physics course. The authors of the present study utilized students' personal mobile computers (laptops and Tablet PCs) in order to capitalize on their productive features in improving student learning in an algebra-based introductory physics course. At the same time, we wanted to minimize possible negative effects. The course was taught in a lecture setting at Columbus State University.

## 3. Solution Employed

In the spring semester of 2010 we invited and encouraged students to bring their wireless computers to physics classes, and we deployed DyKnow software [2] in this course to increase students' active participation in the lecture and to facilitate productive note taking. The main advantages associated with using DyKnow software include [5]: (1) elimination of the need to copy the displayed content, (2) availability of multiple channels of real-time feedback for the instructor, and (3) facilitated group work through simultaneous annotation of slides. DyKnow can be utilized with laptops and Tablet PCs, but unlike laptops, Tablet PCs allow for handwritten electronic inking, which is extremely helpful in areas that use a lot of symbolic annotations such as physics, other STEM fields (science, technology, engineering, and math), and the like.

A disadvantage of applying the software in our setting was that computers were not required, and we relied on students' voluntary participation for bringing wireless ready devices to classes. Expecting mostly laptop computers without inking input, a concern was whether students will be able to use them effectively to take notes in a physics course.

On the first day of classes in spring 2010, the instructor determined that forty-six out of fifty-one present students owned a wireless ready laptop. Shortly thereafter, the number of students who carried their laptop to classes stabilized at around 60 percent of the attendees (and attendance number was typically in the lower to middle forties). This was sufficient to enable a majority of students to capitalize on productive software features and for the instructor to capitalize on a real-time feedback options. In the first half of the semester, four students purchased Tablet PCs and used them consistently in classes.

Formative assessment tools were used throughout the semester. Students with computers were regularly logging into DyKnow and were consistently providing feedback through "status of understanding" feature [3] and multiple-choice answers through the pooling option. Students were also actively submitting slides in response to open-ended questions and problems. Because not all students used computers, it was also necessary to resort to traditional, verbal methods of eliciting questions and other feedback from students. The instructor did not use the monitoring feature of the DyKnow software to control various aspects of students' computers. Therefore, the way in which students utilized their computers was completely up to them. In this setting, we were interested in answering the following research questions: (1) Given possible advantages and disadvantages of using this technology in a voluntary manner, will it be beneficial for students to bring computers to classes? (2) What will be student perceptions of DyKnow facilitated learning in our setting? And (3) given that some students use Tablet PCs, will their performance differ depending on whether they used a laptop or a pen input computer?

## 4. Evaluation

In order to answer these questions, we used several methods: (1) A classroom observation by external evaluator, (2) a comprehensive, end-of-semester online survey that gauged each student's usage patterns and attitude regarding the use of wireless computers and DyKnow in aiding their learning, and (3) a class-wide focus group session run by the same external evaluator. The collected data was examined to determine possible correlations between usage patterns and standard measures of student performance (the test scores and the final grade).

Observational data in the classroom setting did indicate a substantial degree of engagement among the students using computers. Computers facilitated student group work and real-time feedback to the instructor. During the entire class session, only one student with a laptop in use was briefly observed using that laptop for any task that was not related to the class. Students without computers used paper and pencil for note-taking activities typically observed in lecture settings while also participating in group and classroom discussions.

The advantages of this technology that surfaced during the focus group include increased student-student and student-teacher interaction for the whole class, easy reviewing, and the ability to seek content-related input without personal identification if help is needed. Students also found software helpful for organizing notes and helpful to focus on content instead of on note taking. The disadvantages brought up included difficulty with participation if without the computer, difficulty taking notes by hand aside laptop (due to the physical space limitations), the temptation to check e-mail during class, and technical issues.

Out of fifty-three students enrolled in class fourteen days into the semester, thirty-seven took the end-of-semester survey (69.8 percent). One student dropped the course (after the second test), and two more stopped attending halfway through the semester (one of those did take the survey). All survey respondents indicated they personally owned a computer, either a desktop (17), a laptop (29), a Tablet PC (3), or more than one of these types, most frequently a desktop and a laptop (11). Six students owned a desktop only. In Table 1 we compare the patterns of computer usage determined through survey with two measures of student performance: (1) The average scores of the taken tests and (2) the final grade score. For measure (1) only taken tests were included so this indicator is not affected by a missed test. All test questions were standard or slightly modified end-of-the-chapter, open-ended problems typical for algebra-based introductory physics course. The end of the semester score combined the test results (72 percent), (online) homework (22 percent), and (online and class) quizzes (6 percent). The course grade score represents a comprehensive course success, and it would be affected by omitted assignments.

Since our samples were not randomly assigned, we used nonparametric statistic, which gave more conservative results. Thus we used Kruskal-Wallis one-way ANOVA for comparing three and more groups and Mann-Whitney U-test p-values for two group comparison. As shown in Table 1, students who brought computers most frequently to classes performed the best, both in terms of the test scores and overall course grade. However, students who never brought computers performed better than those who brought them in less frequently or occasionally. This might be an indication that students who did not bring computers to class consistently either did not use them effectively or they used computers for activities not related to the course. While differences between respective scores across all categories are not significant, comparison of scores for students who always used computers (category 5) with those who used them less frequently or occasionally (categories 4, 3, 2, 1) show difference significant to 0.05 level both according to average test scores ($p = 0.040$) and according to the course grade

**Table 1.** Computer usage and student success comparisons.

| In spring 2010, on average | Category | All and Each Category | | | Categories 5 vs. 4,3,2,1 | | |
|---|---|---|---|---|---|---|---|
| I was bringing my computer to physics class: | Code | N | Avg. % | SD | N | Avg. % | SD |
| All responses | | 37 | 60.88 | 22.92 | | | |
| Avg. Three times per week (all) | 5 | 21 | 67.49 | 18.20 | 21 | 67.49 | 18.20 |
| Scores Two times per week | 4 | 1 | 10.67 | NA | 8 | 45.03 | 25.80 |
| of Once per week | 3 | 3 | 49.44 | 15.67 | 8 | 45.03 | 25.80 |
| Taken Once or twice per month | 2 | 3 | 48.08 | 37.13 | 8 | 45.03 | 25.80 |
| Tests Once or twice in semester | 1 | 1 | 57.00 | NA | 8 | 45.03 | 25.80 |
| Never | 0 | 8 | 59.39 | 25.85 | | | |
| 1) Kruskal-Wallis and 2) Mann-Whitney test p-values | | | $p=0.365$ | | | $p=0.040$ | |
| I was bringing my computer to physics class: | Code | N | Avg. % | SD | N | Avg. % | SD |
| All responses | | 37 | 72.26 | 22.51 | | | |
| Avg. Three times per week (all) | 5 | 21 | 80.12 | 15.35 | 21 | 80.12 | 15.35 |
| Scores Two times per week | 4 | 1 | 30.17 | NA | 8 | 56.66 | 23.25 |
| of Once per week | 3 | 3 | 59.41 | 18.93 | 8 | 56.66 | 23.25 |
| Taken Once or twice per month | 2 | 3 | 60.19 | 33.51 | 8 | 56.66 | 23.25 |
| Tests Once or twice in semester | 1 | 1 | 64.34 | NA | 8 | 56.66 | 23.25 |
| Never | 0 | 8 | 67.24 | 30.01 | | | |
| 1) Kruskal-Wallis and 2) Mann-Whitney test p-values | | | $p=0.350$ | | | $p=0.019$ | |

scores ($p = 0.019$). The difference strongly favors consistent computer users. Further, when all computer users are compared (with nonusers omitted), bivariate nonparametric correlation (Spearman's Rho) between the computer presence and our two success indicators is significant: at 0.1 level with average test scores ($p = 0.063$) and at 0.05 level with the final grade ($p = 0.028$).

In Table 2 we group students according to their reported cumulative computing activity, which combines a) bringing computers to classes, b) logging on to DyKnow, and c) actively participating in DyKnow-facilitated activities. Students in the "Always" category did all of these three during all the classes. Students in the "Never" category never did any of them (all because they were not bringing computers). "Inconsistent" students fall anywhere in-between the other two. We then compare results of students in these categories with the background measures for students for which both the high school GPA and the SAT math score were present in the university database (math readiness is generally a very good predictor of student success in physics courses). Both of these background data was available for twenty-three students (out of thirty-seven who took the survey), and their results and background scores are shown below.

**Table 2.** Comparison of students' computer and DyKnow activity with success level.

|  |  |  |  | Tests Taken | Course Grade | SAT Math | HS GPA |
|---|---|---|---|---|---|---|---|
| I bring computer | **Always** | **N=7** | Avg | **67.0** | **81.4** | **520.0** | **3.05** |
| AND I log on |  |  | SD | 15.0 | 12.0 | 21.9 | 0.26 |
| to DyKnow | **Inconsistent** | **N=11** | Avg | **57** | **66.8** | **530.9** | **3.38** |
| AND I actively |  |  | SD | 30.3 | 27.5 | 97.9 | 0.43 |
| participate | **Never** | **N=5** | Avg | **58.4** | **67.7** | **500.0** | **3.22** |
|  |  |  | SD | 29.2 | 32.7 | 99.7 | 0.38 |

When these background measures are compared with respect to students' cumulative computing activity (as defined above), we find that among the three student categories it is the inconsistent user group that has both the highest SAT math scores and high school GPA. At the same time this group has the lowest dependent measures scores. Consistent, that is, "Always," users performed better than either of the other two groups in both dependent measures while having the second best SAT math score and the lowest high school GPA. Further details of student performance and their background comparison will be reported elsewhere.

For all thirty-seven participants, this was the first time they used DyKnow. Twenty-eight survey participants reported using it in the classroom, twenty-four at home/dorm, nine on campus, and seven elsewhere outside the campus. Outside the classroom, they reported using DyKnow on average 1.9 hours +/- 1.65 hours per week. Five students never used DyKnow themselves other than experiencing it in classroom. Overall, a large majority of students report positive attitudes about using DyKnow software. However, this attitude very much depends on the type of computer that students used, with Tablet PC users being the most positive. For example, 81 percent of all respondents (N = 37) and 100 percent of Tablet PC users (N = 3) agree or strongly agree that using DyKnow was enjoyable. For 70 percent of all respondents and 100 percent of Tablet PC users, DyKnow enhanced interaction with instructor. The greatest difference between responses of Tablet PC users and all other responses is related to note taking. While all (100 percent) Tablet PC users agree or strongly agree that DyKnow helped them take better notes, only half (51 percent) of all respondents do. The difference in these responses may well be due to the limited space on chair desks used in the classroom; it would be difficult for laptop users to both take notes on paper and use a mobile computer on the desks. It is interesting that five students who did not use DyKnow at all on their personal computers (but rather simply through attending classes in which it was used to enhance interaction) also reported quite positive attitudes toward DyKnow. For 80 percent of them, using DyKnow was enjoyable.

Table 3 breaks answers related to the overall DyKnow experience and recommendations for further usage in this course per Tablet PC using opportunity. It again shows that Tablet PC owners were the most pleased DyKnow users, but those who had a chance to use borrowed Tablet PCs had a better experience and higher recommendations than other users. Students who did not have a chance to use Tablet PCs were not asked about their experience with them but were asked for recommendations based on seeing others (the instructor and other students) using Tablet PCs. Again, unlike nonusers, Tablet PC users highly recommend them, with average recommendation differences between the user groups significant at 0.1 level (p = 0.057, Kruskal-Wallis ANOVA).

**Table 3.** DyKnow and Tablet PC experience and recommendations for usage in physics course.

| | Category | | | DyKnow | | | Tablet PC | |
|---|---|---|---|---|---|---|---|---|
| | | Code | N | Avg. % | SD | N | Avg. % | SD |
| **Overall Experience** — Did you have an opportunity to use a Tablet PC, either yours or borrowed, in Physics I this semester? | | | | | | | | |
| | All responses | | 37 | 3.51 | 1.17 | 6 | 4.33 | 0.52 |
| | Yes, I used my personal Tablet PC | 2 | 3 | 4.33 | 0.58 | 3 | 4.67 | 0.58 |
| | Yes, I used a borrowed Tablet PC | 1 | 3 | 3.67 | 0.58 | 3 | 4.00 | 0.00 |
| | No, I did not use a Tablet PC | 0 | 31 | 3.42 | 1.23 | NA | NA | NA |
| | Kruskal-Wallis ANOVA p-values | | | p=0.404 | | | p=0.114 | |
| | Category | Code | N | Avg. % | SD | N | Avg. % | SD |
| **Recommendations for this course** — Did you have an opportunity to use a Tablet PC, either yours or borrowed, in Physics I this semester? | | | | | | | | |
| | All responses | | 37 | 3.57 | 1.26 | 37 | 3.51 | 1.17 |
| | Yes, I used my personal Tablet PC | 2 | 3 | 4.67 | 0.58 | 3 | 4.67 | 0.58 |
| | Yes, I used a borrowed Tablet PC | 1 | 3 | 4.00 | 0.00 | 3 | 4.33 | 0.58 |
| | No, I did not use a Tablet PC | 0 | 31 | 3.42 | 1.31 | 31 | 3.32 | 1.17 |
| | Kruskal-Wallis ANOVA p-values | | | p=0.176 | | | p=0.057 | |

In Table 4 we compare test performance and course success of students who used different computer types. Both of these measures show that Tablet PC users performed much better than either laptop or desktop (only) users. The difference between Tablet PC users and all other survey respondents is significant at 0.1 level (p = 0.059 for test scores and p = 0.095 for the course grade).

**Table 4.** Computer type used and student success comparisons.

| | | Category | All and Each Category | | | Categories 3 vs 2,1,0 | | |
|---|---|---|---|---|---|---|---|---|
| | | Code | N | Avg. % | SD | N | Avg. % | SD |
| | All responses | | 37 | 60.88 | 22.92 | | | |
| Avg. | Tablet | 3 | 3 | 81.03 | 3.88 | 3 | 81.03 | 3.88 |
| Scores | Laptop | 2 | 28 | 60.25 | 21.32 | 34 | 59.10 | 23.06 |
| of | Desktop | 1 | 6 | 53.75 | 31.84 | 34 | 59.10 | 23.06 |
| Taken | None | 0 | 0 | NA | NA | 34 | 59.10 | 23.06 |
| Tests | 1) Kruskal-Wallis and 2) Mann-Whitney test p-values | | | p=0.162 | | | p=0.059 | |

| The top mobile computer I own | | Code | N | Avg. % | SD | N | Avg. % | SD |
|---|---|---|---|---|---|---|---|---|
| | All responses | | 37 | 72.26 | 22.51 | | | |
| Course | Tablet | 3 | 3 | 90.72 | 2.69 | 3 | 90.72 | 2.69 |
| Grade | Laptop | 2 | 28 | 72.80 | 19.58 | 34 | 70.63 | 22.78 |
| Result | Desktop | 1 | 6 | 60.54 | 34.72 | 34 | 70.63 | 22.78 |
| | None | 0 | 0 | NA | NA | 34 | 70.63 | 22.78 |
| | 1) Kruskal-Wallis and 2) Mann-Whitney test p-values | | | p=0.244 | | | p=0.095 | |

In conclusion, when a computer-facilitated active learning experience is provided, consistent wireless-computer classroom users are likely to benefit from it more than nonusers. However, inconsistent and sporadic users are likely harmed by the availability of the computer. Therefore, ways of controlling the off-the-task computer usage, possibly such as DyKnow monitor are necessary to prevent harmful effects of inconsistent and off-the-task usage. Among consistent users, Tablet PC owners surpass the laptop users both in terms of class performance and the satisfaction with technology. This is likely due to the ease of taking notes with the Tablet PC. Overall, with consistent use and adequate control of misusage, wireless laptops (and especially Tablet PCs) in classrooms are likely to be an asset rather than disadvantage for students.

## 4. Acknowledgments

This work was supported in part by DyKnow Inc.

## References

[1] Barak, M., Lipson, A., and Lerman, S. Wireless Laptops as Means for Promoting Active Learning in Large Lecture Halls. *Journal of Research on Technology in Education*, 38 (2006) 245-263.

[2] DyKnow. Dyknow Vision and Monitor. *Vol. 2010*, 2007.

[3] Fort Hays State University. DyKnow Video Contest. 2010.

[4] Fried, C. B. In-class laptop use and its effects on student learning. *Computers & Education*, 50 (2008) 906-914.

[5] Hrepic, Z., Rebello, N. S., and Zollman, D. A. Remedying Shortcomings of Lecture-Based Physics Instruction Through Pen-Based, Wireless Computing And DyKnow Software. In N. H. Salas and D. D. Peyton (Eds.). *Reading: Assessment, Comprehension and Teaching*, Nova Science Publishers; reprinted in Journal of Education Research, 3(1/2) (2009) 161-190. (2009) 97-129.

[6] Mortkowitz, L. More colleges, professors shutting down laptops and other digital distractions. *The Washington Post*, 2010.

[7] Sisson, C. J. Tablet-based recitations in Physics: Less lecture, more success. In D. A. Berque, L. M. Konkle, and R. H. Reed (Eds.). *The Impact of Tablet PCs and Pen-based Technology on Education: New Horizons*, Purdue University Press, 2009, 133-139.

# INK-12: A Pen-based Wireless Classroom Interaction System for K-12

*Kimberle Koile,[1] David Reider,[2] and Andee Rubin[3]*

[1]*MIT Center for Educational Computing Initiatives,* [2]*Education Design, Inc.,*
*and* [3]*TERC*

## 1. Abstract

This paper describes research conducted in the two-year NSF-funded INK-12: Interactive Ink Inscriptions in K-12 research project. In this project, we have been investigating the role that pen-based wireless technology could play in upper elementary and middle school science and math. We have conducted Tablet PC computing trials in eight schools in the Boston, Massachusetts, area—six fourth, one sixth, and three eighth grade teachers' classrooms, working with a total of four hundred students. During each of these trials, the project team helped teachers adapt their lessons to make best use of the Tablet PCs and to think strategically about pacing the lesson, accommodating different types of learners, and dealing with unexpected technological challenges. The Tablet PCs were particularly successful in (1) facilitating students' creation of drawings and other mathematical and scientific representations and (2) providing teachers with tools to promote classroom discussions. The research identified areas that need further work, including providing a more flexible metaphor than "slides" for lessons and student submissions, and designing professional development to support teachers in choosing appropriate student work for class discussion.

## 2. Problem Statement and Context

In the two-year exploratory INK-12 research project, we have been investigating how the combination of two technological innovations—pen-based input and wireless communication—can support and transform classroom practices and student learning in K-12 science, technology, engineering, and mathematics (STEM) disciplines. In particular, we have been investigating how the technology can enhance the teaching and learning of mathematics and science by (1) giving students enhanced capabilities to *create and manipulate* representations of mathematical and scientific objects and (2) providing facilities for *communicating* representations that can support conversation among teachers and students about science and mathematics content. *Pen-based* interaction enables the creation of *inscriptions*—handwritten sketches, graphs, maps, notes, and so on, which are critical in STEM fields, where content is often most easily expressed as a mixture of text and drawings. Teachers and students can easily draw and write on a Tablet PC's screen (create "ink" inscriptions), thereby extending the representations possible with only the typical keyboard and mouse or pencil and paper. *Wireless* networking enables facile communication of inscriptions, and other representations, among teachers and students. The communication provides a teacher the opportunity to look at all her students' work at the same time on her Tablet PC and makes possible discussions based on selections of student work that can be made visible to all students and the teacher simultaneously. In this way, the technology can support a "conversation-based" classroom in which students discuss their reasoning and listen critically to others' reasoning. Such conversations provide valuable opportunities for feedback to both students and teachers, feedback that can be used to improve both learning and teaching.

## 3. Solution Employed

The technology used in the trials consists of a set of Tablet PCs running a software system called Classroom Learning Partner (CLP), developed by the first author's research group [3, 4, 5]. CLP is built on top of the wireless presentation system Classroom Presenter [1, 2]. Classroom Presenter provides the underlying wireless communication, as well as much of the user interface's functionality and style, both of which are very intuitive. Like Classroom Presenter, CLP embodies a "presentation slide" metaphor for classroom interaction: A teacher creates a lesson as a series of PowerPoint slides. In the classroom, the teacher and students all have Tablet PCs on which the lesson is running; the lesson also is projected on a large public screen. The teacher can annotate a displayed slide by using the

Tablet PC's stylus to create digital ink, which, by way of a wireless network, is then visible on the students' and public screens. Students, in turn, can write on their Tablet PC screens and send the digital ink to their teacher, for example, as answers to in-class exercises. The teacher then can select some, or all, of those answers to display on the public screen and engage students in class discussion. Examples of student work from our research are shown below in Figure 1.

**Figure 1.** Fourth grade (top) and eighth grade (bottom) student work.

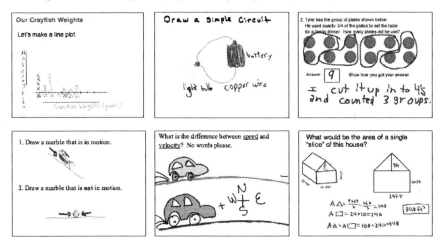

The current version of CLP extends Classroom Presenter in the following ways.

*Classroom setup*: We run CLP using a classroom server and local peer-to-peer network, which is automatically established as soon as the Tablet PCs are started up. With this setup we avoid using school networks, which are often unreliable and without on-site technical support. We automated much of the software start-up procedure so that teachers and students (1) only use the Tablet pC pen, not the keyboard, and (2) spend very little time initiating a lesson. Teachers and students start the software by tapping on an icon on the Tablet PC desktop; the software connects to the peer-to-peer network, retrieves the lesson from the server, and connects to the current classroom session. When the students start CLP, a log-in window pops up, allowing them to choose their names from a class list, which is populated from data retrieved from the server. The log-in information is used for storing student submissions on the server, and for labeling submissions so that teachers can match submissions with students—a feature that we found K-12 teachers needed, especially to respond to requests from students to "show mine."

*Teacher's features:* We implemented a number of features that facilitate the teacher's use of student work as a basis for classroom conversation. Student submissions are organized by slide on the teacher's machine, with one submission deck per slide. The teacher has easy access to submissions via a tab associated with his or her version of each slide. Figure 2a shows a teacher's screen, with her lesson slides in the vertical filmstrip on the left; CLP's gray tab on the right of a slide indicates the presence of submissions, and the number on the left indicates the number of students who have sent submissions. Tapping on the tab displays the student submissions for that slide in the filmstrip; tapping on a particular submission slide in the filmstrip displays it on the both the teacher and public machines. Tapping on the "multidisplay" icon at the top of the filmstrip enables the teacher to select submissions to display simultaneously on the public machine—another feature that teachers found enhanced their ability to hold class conversations about multiple representations and problem-solving approaches. An example of creating a multidisplay is below in Figure 2.b-d: Student work is "stacked" and displayed in a filmstrip on the left, one stack per student; the teacher expands stacks as desired, by clicking on a student's name on a stack, and drags submissions onto a "stage," then selects column or grid view.

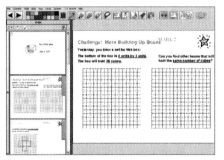

**Figure 2.a.** Selects slide, then taps multidisplay icon.

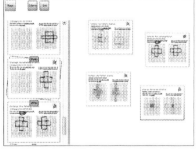

**b.** Drags submissions; yellow shows one chosen.

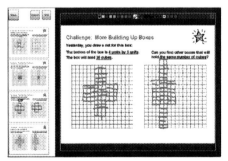

**c.** Can select Column and "zoom" in on work.

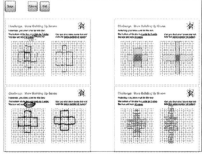

**d.** Can select Grid view to display all chosen.

We also added a feature that enables the teacher to send ink only to the projector, not both public and student machines—students wanted to see the teacher's annotations on the public screen, but most became incensed when the teacher's ink showed up on their slides! We added features that enable the teacher to privately view, annotate student submissions, and send the annotated slides back to students without other students seeing her comments.

*Student's features:* We made three changes to the elementary student's view of the screen. Specifically, we added a color palette, which we also incorporated into the teacher's view; removed distracting commands (lasso, highlighter, erase all); and added a history panel, which students can hide or reveal, that enables them to view and restore their submissions and to view messages from their teacher (see Figure 3). For middle school students, we only removed the highlighter, which, although useful, proves distracting even for adults.

**Figure 3.** Student view; history shows current slide (far left), submissions, teacher message (far right).

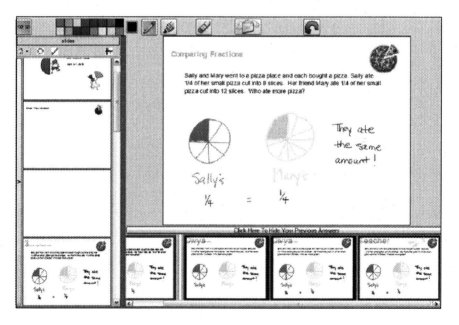

## 4. Evaluation

The INK-12 project team has conducted Tablet PC computing trials in eight schools—six fourth, one sixth, and three eighth grade teachers' classrooms, working with a total of four hundred students.

**Table 1.** Schedule of our classroom trials from fall 2008 to spring 2010 in fourth, sixth, and eighth grade classrooms.

| School System/School | Grade | Length of time | Class size | Topics |
|---|---|---|---|---|
| Lexington/Fiske | 4 | 1 day | 22 | Graphing scientific data |
| Lexington/Bridge | 4 | 1 day | 23 | Graphing scientific data |
| Cambridge/Baldwin | 4 | 4 days | 18 | Math, test prep for math & language arts state tests |
| Cambridge/Baldwin | 4 | 4 days | 18 | Math, test prep for math & language arts state tests |
| Lexington/Clarke | 8 | 5 days/5 classes each day | 20 | Physics |
| Lexington/Clarke | 8 | 5 days/5 classes each day | 20 | Algebra |
| Cambridge/Amigos | 8 | 3 days/2 classes each day | 22 | Algebra |
| Waltham/Northeast | 4 | two 3-day trials | 20 | Math (fractions), science |
| Waltham/Kennedy | 6 | 3 days/4 classes each day | 21 | Science |
| Newton/Cabot | 4 | 3 days | 23 | Math |

## 4.1 Study Design

During each of these trials, the project team helped teachers adapt their lessons to make best use of the Tablet PCs; in most cases, the teachers did not deviate from their planned lessons, but rather extended and deepened them using the Tablet PC capabilities. Project staff helped teachers think strategically about pacing the lesson, accommodating different types of learners, and dealing with unexpected technological challenges. Teachers needed the most help planning how to choose and use student work; they needed support in both technological aspects (how to navigate the student submission system) and pedagogical considerations (how to choose appropriate work examples).

Data collection included formal observation of classes using an observation protocol, post-residency interview with participating teachers, student focus group discussions, inventory analysis of student work samples, and student evaluations collected at end of residencies.

## 4.2 Classroom Observations

The following classroom behaviors were encoded and included in the analyses: lecture, demonstration, lecture with discussion, class discussion, small group discussion, teacher interacting with student, Tablet PC technology use, hands-on activity (non-computer), revising work, sending/receiving wireless data, interruption, passive learning, and active learning.

Overall, our findings suggest that students were highly engaged (85 percent of the time). They also suggest that INK-12 Tablet PC sessions provide ample classroom opportunities for interactive instructional methods (lecture with discussion), increased communication and feedback (send/receiving wireless data), and engaging students in active learning. Students adapted quickly to the Tablet PC interface; very little class time was spent in technology training or support.

### 4.3 Teacher Reflections

Teachers felt that the Tablet PCs were easy to use from the beginning; most had less than thirty minutes of training and quickly adapted their teaching style to instruct with the Tablet PCs. They unanimously reported that students were motivated to use the Tablet PCs to try activities normally completed with paper and pencil. The teachers felt that Tablet PC use changed the way the teaching and learning occurred in their classrooms, but were reluctant to postulate that student outcomes, retention, or performance improved as a result of using the technology. All teachers, however, felt that they wanted to continue using the equipment and to develop more sophisticated and longer curriculum units in order to investigate how student learning is affected. All teachers felt that increased student engagement, focus, questioning, and work completion as a result of Tablet PC use directly led to increased active student participation in the learning process, which they felt, if continued, would result in improved outcomes. Several teachers identified ways they saw the Tablet PCs providing options for teaching a lesson, providing a variety of entry points for different kinds of learners, for example, those who like technology, like communicating, do not like writing but like drawing, are shy, are slower, or who typically do not complete assignments.

### 4.4 Student Comments

Students were asked to respond to questions related to their experiences with the Tablet PCs. The greatest number of student comments mentioned the assets of receiving fast feedback from the teacher, ease of erasing on the Tablet PC, varied visual representations possible with the colors and pen shapes, how they thought the technology helped cover more material than they normally did, and the importance of seeing other students' answers publicly. In addition, when we asked if they preferred to have their name on their publicly displayed work, 78 percent of those who responded said either yes or that it did not matter; 22 percent responded that they preferred anonymity.

### 4.5 Summary

Overall, students seemed very engaged, not just during the first "novelty" moments, and excitement resulted in increased participation. The drawing component provided an alternative input to handwriting or typing, and proved popular and successful with all kinds of students, especially those who were struggling learners. Student sharing of work provided a classroom context that invited discussion and student-led explanations. Teachers were unanimously enthusiastic about using and developing lessons specifically for the Tablet PCs. They suggested features, improvements, and thought of many potential uses beyond those specified by the project. All felt to some extent that wider and longer-term use was possible within their classrooms, and would be eager to continue trialing the technology should the opportunity arise.

What we have learned from teachers and students is that the INK-12 Tablet PC environment has much to offer classrooms, at both the elementary and middle school grade levels. Classroom learning characteristics represent many of those associated with project-based learning, interactive instruction, active learning, and inquiry-based learning. Students respond well, in particular to those elements social in nature, for example, publicly sharing work and communicating with the teacher via wireless networking.

We also learned that several issues need further work. The slide metaphor was too restrictive at times. Students sometimes needed more answer space than provided by one slide; an electronic notebook metaphor may prove more appropriate. At times teachers wanted students to be able to construct representations that were more accurate than could be drawn by hand, for example, an equilateral triangle. In addition, teachers found it challenging to select student work for public display; some chose randomly, others chose by student, some felt more comfortable looking at student work after class and displaying student work the following day.

## 5. Future Work

The project team has just been awarded a four-year NSF grant to continue studying the use of INK-12 technology in K-12 classrooms. The upcoming work will target upper elementary math and science, and will focus on (1) developing the technology while monitoring teacher and student responses in order to inform the development process; and (2) collecting data as empirical evidence about such technology's effect on teaching and learning in K-12 STEM education.

## 6. Acknowledgments

This research was funded by NSF DRK-12 collaborative awards DRL-0822278 (Koile), DRL-0822055 (Rubin); many thanks to program officer Michael Haney for his support. The PIs gratefully acknowledge the contributions from members of the MIT CLP research group: Steve Diles, Neil Chao, Martyna Jozwiak, Brandon Pung, Brian Wheeler, and William Gaviria. At TERC, we thank Swapna Reddy and Tracey Wright for classroom and logistical support.

# References

[1] Anderson, R., et. al. Experiences with a Tablet PC Based Lecture Presentation System in Computer Science Courses. In *Proceedings of SIGCSE* 2004. http://classroompresenter. cs.washington.edu/.

[2] Anderson, R., et. al. Classroom Presenter: Enhancing Interactive Education with Digital Ink. *Computer*. Los Alamitos, CA, IEEE Computer Society, 40, 9 (Sept. 2007) 56-61.

[3] Koile K., et. al. Supporting Feedback and Assessment of Digital Ink Answers to In-Class Exercises. In *Proceedings of IAAI 2007*.

[4] Koile, K., et al. Supporting Pen-Based Classroom Interaction: New Findings and Functionality for Classroom Learning Partner. In *Proceedings of the First International Workshop on Pen-Based Learning Technologies 2007*.

[5] Koile, K., and Singer, D. Assessing the Impact of a Tablet-PC-based Classroom Interaction System. In *Proceedings of WIPTE 2008*.

# Is Tablet-based Teaching for Everyone?
# An Exploration of Teaching with Tablet PCs
# across Science and Humanities Classes

*Murray Logan, Katharina Franke, and Nathan Bailey*

*Monash University*

## 1. Abstract

Tablet PCs have been extensively explored in science, engineering, and computer science education, and to a lesser extent in medicine, business, and economics (cf. [2, 5]). However, there is relatively little literature on their potential and impact within the humanities. This study examines and contrasts student usage and perceptions of Tablet PCs in a science cohort (biology) and two humanities cohorts (history and philosophy).

The experiences reported by students in a first year philosophy course were found to be similarly positive to those offered by a third year biology cohort, suggesting that these technologies and pedagogies have the potential to facilitate more interactive and engaging teaching and learning environments across a range of disciplines and year levels. Nevertheless, the degree of utilization and perceived usefulness of Tablet PCs in learning spaces appeared proportional to the degree to which teaching staff use and adopt the technologies. Biology and philosophy lectures made more substantial and consistent use of Classroom Presenter 3 software than did the instructors in the history course, and they were associated with greater reported student Tablet PC usage and higher perceived value.

## 2. Problem Statement and Context

Tablet PCs are increasingly being utilized at universities in Australia as a medium to encourage more flexibility in content delivery, to create a sense of spontaneity, and to a lesser extent, to allow student-instructor interaction. Monash University has been moving toward more engaging models of education, involving collaborative software and Tablet PCs, since 2008 (see [4] for more details).

Tablet PCs provide an opportunity to visually collaborate around learning materials, thus lending themselves very well to disciplines that examine facts, figures, and visually-oriented information that can be circled, highlighted, annotated, and quizzed upon. Accordingly, it is still mostly science-orientated courses, including engineering, computer science, and medicine that have taken advantage of teaching and learning with pen-based technology (cf., for example, the papers in [2], all of which deal with Tablet PC-based teaching in science-orientated courses) with only limited exploration in a humanities context (e.g. [3, 6]). While the humanities may also incorporate factual knowledge and visual artifacts, generally their teaching approaches focus on key principles, major concepts, and the big picture in a manner in which detailed analyses and annotation represent only minor components of the in-class experience.

Hence, while Tablet PCs have demonstrable benefits and pedagogical foundations within disciplines that are more driven by factual and logical patterns, it is unclear whether these technologies and methodologies can be successfully applied to more conceptual and abstract disciplines and the students they attract. This paper explores how the experiences of students with Tablet PC-based teaching and learning in humanities cohorts compare with a science cohort.

## 3. Solution Employed

Following from the success of Tablet PC-based teaching trials conducted in 2008 and comprising of first, second, and third year biology courses, the myLearningSpace program[1] was extended in 2009 to include two humanities courses (PHL1140—"Introducing Logic" and HSY1010—"Medieval Europe") in addition to one of the original biology courses (BIO3011—"Research Methods in Biology"). Table 1 provides further details on the student cohorts.

While the BIO3011 and HSY1010 courses were selected to represent either end of a science-history (logical-rhetorical) spectrum, the philosophy course was strategically selected so as to represent a largely humanities cohort partaking in science-like, logic-based activities. It was hoped that this would provide an avenue to uncouple the impact of student discipline preference versus course matter on Tablet PC usage patterns and perceptions.

**Table 1.** Overview of the teaching cohorts participating in the myLearning-Space program, 2009. *Full enrollment ninety-two. Forty-two additional students were randomly selected to take part in a comparison program in which they experienced two different Tablet PC models (see [4] for details) and were thus excluded from the present study.

| | BIO3011 – 3rd Yr "Research Methods in Biology" | PHL1140 – 1st Yr "Introducing Logic" | HSY1010 –1st Yr "Medieval Europe" |
|---|---|---|---|
| Discipline | Science (biology) | Humanities (philosophy) | Humanities (history) |
| Semester | Sem 1, 2009 | Sem 2, 2009 | Sem 1, 2009 |
| Student enrollment | 50* | 92 | 190 |
| Course content (per week) | 2x1hr lecture 1x3hr practical | 2x1hr lecture 1x1hr tutorial | 2x1hr lecture 1x1hr tutorial |
| Instructor details | One instructor | Two instructors | One main instructor + guest instructors |
| Presentation software | CP3 Extensive use of interactive features | CP3 Extensive use of interactive features | CP3 + PowerPoint Limited use of interactive features |

At the start of the semester, students enrolled in the participating courses were provided with a custom-imaged Fujitsu LifeBook (P1630 or P1610) Tablet PC, including 3G access for engaging in learning activities off-campus. Students were invited to treat the device as their own for the duration of the semester.

Lectures in all three courses were predominantly delivered through the active use of Classroom Presenter 3 (CP3) software [1], making use of interactive features such as slide submission and quizzes, in a networked environment in which students could choose to use their Tablet PC to follow the presentation slides as well as to take electronic notes using either their stylus or the mouse and keyboard (see Figure 1d). Similarly, CP3 was also used in PHL1140 tutorials to facilitate diverse interactive opportunities. The BIO3011 practical laboratory sessions focused on applied experimental design and statistical data analysis, thereby necessitating the use of specialist computer software in addition to the collaboration software. In these practical sessions, students could elect to use either their Tablet PC or an existing laboratory computer station.

While students from each of the cohorts were permitted to use the Tablet PCs inside and outside of formal classes (including courses not participating in the myLearningSpace program) for homework, library study, group collaboration, and personal use, they were under no obligation to bring their Tablet PCs to teaching events, or indeed to ever use them for any purpose.

## 4. Evaluation

In order to evaluate student perceptions and usage patterns across different learning domains, an online survey was conducted at the end of each semester. Of the 50 participating BIO3011, 92 PHL1140, and 190 HSY1010 students, 33 (66 percent), 31 (34 percent), and 35 (18 percent), respectively, responded to the survey.

The current study sits within a much broader exploration of Tablet PC-based teaching and learning at Monash University, and therefore, the survey asked students to reflect on a wide range of issues relating to the myLearningSpace program. The focus for this paper is on Tablet PC usage patterns and perceived learning benefits during structured teaching and learning events (lectures, practicals, and tutorials) as these are the domains generally identified as in need of the greatest innovation and modernization in order to remain relevant in the current and future scholastic climates. Nevertheless, summations of usage patterns and perceptions across other learning domains will be presented graphically for the purpose of perspective.

### 4.1 Student Usage Patterns and Perceptions across Learning Domains

On average, BIO3011 students indicated significantly greater Tablet PC usage (Figure 1a) than either HSY1010 or PHL1140 students. As this pattern occurred across all learning domains (except lectures), it is likely that this outcome reflects the greater emphasis on, and need for, computer-based learning materials and assessment tasks expected of students enrolled in BIO3011 given the nature of the course (experimental design and statistical analysis) as well as the year level. Furthermore, the higher usage of Tablet PCs in BIO3011 may also be the result of the instructor's engagement and familiarity with the technology considering his previous experience with Tablet PC-based teaching.

In the surveys, BIO3011 and PHL1140 students occasionally commented on the tendency of instructors to construct ideas more dynamically and interactively within CP3 (Figure 1c), thereby giving students the ability to contribute to the construction of the lesson, or if not, at least to witness the evolution of ideas into synthesised points. By contrast, PowerPoint tends to be used to present facts in an already prepackaged format where students are not privy to the genesis and derivations. It is not always obvious to instructors that the genesis is the most important element of learning—the software used should allow, if not encourage, this process. On the other hand, some HSY1010 students lamented that their perceptions of CP3 and the values of Tablet PCs could have been affected by issues with hardware and inconsistent academic adoption. At the same time, student reasons for preferring PowerPoint were somewhat peripheral and included the ability to print slides and notes, hardware issues, and file formats.

## 4.2 Lecture Domain

Importantly, no such differences were found between usage patterns of BIO3011 and PHL1140 students within their respective focal lectures (see Figure 1a). Furthermore, despite clear discrepancies across the practical-tutorial domains, the benefits of Tablet PC-based teaching perceived by students in a lecture context are very consistent between the BIO3011 and PHL1140 cohorts (Figure 1b).

**Figure 1.** Comparison of Tablet PC a) mean (±SE) usage ("How often did you use your Tablet PC at university?"); b) percentage student perceived benefits ("Using my Tablet PC in class benefited . . ."); c) student preferred software ("Given a choice I would prefer . . ."); and d) modes of Tablet PC input ("How did you use your Tablet PC in class?") across a range of teaching and learning domains by biology, philosophy, and history cohorts. *Denotes focal courses (BIO3011, PHL1140, and HYS1010).

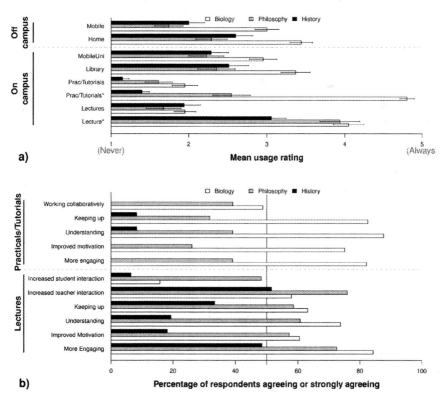

*Figure 1. Continued.*

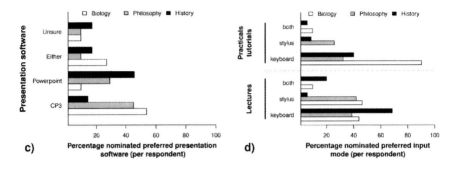

c) **Percentage nominated preferred presentation software (per respondent)**

d) **Percentage nominated preferred input mode (per respondent)**

These students also portray similarly strong preferences for CP3 lecture delivery over either PowerPoint or no preference at all (Figure 1c), and report to predominantly use either the stylus for electronic note taking or the keyboard in lectures (but rarely a mixture of both; see Figure 1d). These similarities potentially indicate that students in the humanities are as capable and willing to embrace Tablet PC-based technologies and associated teaching approaches as are science students.

Mean Tablet PC usage in focal lectures reported by HSY1010 students was, however, significantly less than that of either BIO3011 or PHL1140 students (Figure 1a). Accordingly, students enrolled in HSY1010 were also less convinced that the use of Tablet PCs improved their educational experience (Figure 1b); they preferred the more traditional PowerPoint lecture delivery where the instructor inked directly on PowerPoint slides, and they predominantly used the keyboard and mouse for taking notes during lectures (Figures 1c-d). The contrasting behaviors and attitudes of students enrolled in HSY1010 (despite having been drawn from a similar student pool as the students enrolled in PHL1140) might suggest that the nature of the course matter (more so than the characteristics of the individual students) determines the usefulness of the explored technologies and pedagogies.

Alternatively, these divergent lecture experiences could represent an extension of the more general patterns that emerge in Tablet PC usage and perceptions across a range of learning domains. The patterns seem to indicate that the extent of student Tablet PC usage and positivity of attitudes toward tablet PC-based teaching in classes may be proportional to the degree to which teaching staff use and employ the technologies (see Figures 1a-b, in addition to Table 1).

Indeed—unlike BIO3011 or PHL1140—the weekly HSY1010 lectures alternated between the main instructor and, in most weeks, a series of guest instructors who employed Tablet PC-based teaching only to a limited extent, if at all. In addition, HSY1010 was marred by technology problems in the first five weeks of the semester, essentially due to instability with CP3 and wireless infrastructure. To avoid further disruptions during lectures, interactive features, such as polling and slide submissions, were used only infrequently. The main instructor, however, continued to annotate slides, using CP3 or PowerPoint, throughout the semester.

### 4.3 Practicals and Tutorials Domain

The greatest discrepancy in reported Tablet PC usage occurred within the practicals/tutorials (see Figure 1a). In particular, on average, BIO3011 students indicated that they almost always used their Tablet PCs in practicals (which were very computer-intensive), whereas usage of Tablet PCs in tutorials of HSY1010 and PHL1140 students was very low (in fact, lower than in lectures). Moreover, students were considerably less convinced of the improvements to learning that Tablet PCs could bring to the tutorial domain than to lectures (Figure 1b). Tutorials are typically less populous and inherently more interactive than lectures and science practicals. Perhaps students did not perceive it necessary to use a Tablet PC in order to achieve interactivity and feedback in tutorials, and their comparatively high use and commendation of Tablet PCs in lectures reflects a greater desire and effort to obtain interactivity and feedback in lectures.

## 5. Conclusion

Student perspectives suggest that Tablet PC technologies and associated constructionist pedagogies do offer similar opportunities to those already heralded and investigated more widely within the science-based disciplines. Nevertheless, the degree of utilization and perceived usefulness of Tablet PCs in teaching and learning spaces is clearly proportional to the degree to which teaching staff use and adopt the technologies in pedagogically meaningful ways. BIO3011 and PHL1140 lectures made more substantial and consistent use of CP3's annotation capabilities and interactive features, and were associated with greater reported student Tablet PC usage as well as perceived value.

## 6. Future Work

While students do perceive Tablet PC-based teaching and learning as enhancing engagement, motivation, and interactivity with instructors, the currently available presentation applications fail to harness the pedagogical merits of student-student collaborations, peer sourcing, and networking. Our current research addresses these powerful yet complex issues with a project that extends the scope of synchronicity and interactivity across all students simultaneously in a manner analogous to popular social networking and communication protocols.

## 7. Additional Resources

eEducation Centre homepage: monash.edu/eEducation. To find out more about the myLearningSpace program, visit monash.edu/eEducation/myLS2010.

## 8. Acknowledgments

The authors would like to acknowledge the instructors of the HSY1010, Clare Monagle, and the PHL1140, Sam Butchart and Monima Chadha, for their enthusiasm to explore the myLearningSpace educational approach, and for their contributions to this paper.

## Notes

1    The myLearningSpace program is an initiative that encourages more engaging peda-gogical approaches based on the use of Tablet PCs and collaborative software. It explores the potentials and impacts of technologies and spaces on teaching and learning. For more information, see monash.edu/eEducation/myLS2010.

## References

[1] Anderson, R. University of Washington Classroom Presenter, University of Washington, http://classroompresenter.cs.washington.edu/.

[2] Berque, D. A., Konkle, L. M., and Reed, R. H. (Eds.). *The Impact of Tablet PCs and Pen-based Technology on Education: New Horizons*. Purdue University Press, 2009.

[3] Itoh, R. Use of handwriting input in writing instruction for Japanese language. In D. A. Berque, J. C. Prey, and R. H. Reed (Eds.). *The Impact of Tablet PCs and Pen-based Technology on Education: Vignettes, Evaluations, and Future Directions*. Purdue University Press, 2006, 87-93.

[4] Logan, M., Bailey, N., Franke, K., and Sanson, G. Patterns of Tablet PC use across multiple learning domains: A comparison program. In D. A. Berque, L. M. Konkle, and R. H. Reed (Eds.). *The Impact of Tablet PCs and Pen-based Technology on Education: New horizons*. Purdue University Press, 2009, 83-92.

[5] Reed, R. H., Berque, D. A., and Prey, J. C. (Eds.). *The Impact of Tablet PCs and Pen-based Technology on Education: Evidence and Outcomes*. Purdue University Press, 2008.

[6] Snodgrass, J. S. Seeing the big picture: How the Tablet PC creates an engaging classroom experience. In R. H. Reed, D. A. Berque, and J. C. Prey (Eds.). *The Impact of Tablet PCs and Pen-based Technology on Education: Evidence and Outcomes*. Purdue University Press, 2008, 137-144.

# Developing a Learning Support System for Students in Mathematics Rich Disciplines

*Anne Porter and Norhayati Baharun*

*University of Wollongong*

## 1. Abstract

This paper focuses on two aspects of an Australian Learning and Teaching Council-funded project, "Building Leadership Capacity in the Development and Sharing of Mathematics Learning Resources, Across Disciplines, Across Universities." The primary aim of this project is to develop leadership capacity, which in the simplest sense is to engage others in the sharing of predominantly Tablet PC-created video mathematics learning resources. The resources were to cover 100-level tertiary mathematics, statistics, and bridging programs, and thereby higher levels of university courses in the disciplines that used 100-level mathematics and statistics. The sharing of technical expertise in relation to creation of resources has been one of the successes of this project as has the development and trial of different genres of video. The Tablet PC has been the major tool used to create resources. The creation of resources has led to questions as to the best ways to combine resources and hence the second focus on *learning design* for effective learning support of mathematics-based courses.

## 2. Problem Statement and Context

Teaching disciplines that have mathematics as a fundamental component are fraught with difficulties, worldwide. The decline in levels of mathematics courses taken by high school students in Australia has been well documented [5]. The lowering of contact hours, entry standards, student ability, and engagement with mathematics poses problems at the tertiary level not only in the study of mathematics, but in disciplines such as engineering where mathematics skills are considered to be of fundamental importance.

A wide range of approaches to the provision of mathematics learning support have been identified [9]. In the Australian context, several universities have no mathematics learning support center. Others have lone workers. At the other extreme, there are universities that have a solid core of mathematics learning support. Characteristic of many universities that have such support are restrictions of resources to bridging courses or 100-level students. Sometimes support is restricted to small group work as opposed to individual tuition, reflecting the limit of resources. Diversity in levels of support has been identified and is often closely related to the strategic priorities given to mathematics support in universities. Also characteristic of many of the descriptions in the report is dominance of two or three disciplines from which students are drawn and from which the service is potentially funded.

Participants at the symposium on Learning Support for Mathematics and Statistics (QUT, July 2007) recognized:

• The critical roles of mathematical and statistical skills in underpinning student success in many courses

• The need to care for students entering with diverse mathematics backgrounds and skills

• The need for learning support in mathematics and statistics to provide a range of services tailored for needs of relevant courses, circumstances, and cohorts

• The difficulties of meeting increasing student needs in mathematics and statistics with uncertain funding, stretched personnel, and scarce space [7]

## 3. Solution Employed

In developing a learning support system, one core component of the solution has involved the development of video-based learning support resources that may be used within mathematics learning centers or be embedded within courses'

Web sites. The dominant genre for our project has been the "worked example" with a typed question followed by handwritten solutions with voice-over. Other genres, illustrated theory clips, capture of statistical and mathematical software operation, expert-novice discussion of examples, and expert-expert discussion of alternative solutions have also been created. Research into the use of worked examples, completion examples, and practice examples has found that novices can learn quicker, with fewer training and test errors when provided with worked examples rather than practice examples [6]. The Tablet PC has been crucial in the development of resources. Surrounding this core objective are many issues that need to be addressed from different perspectives: nationally, institutionally, at faculty level (across degree programs), at a school level, and at course level.

### 3.1 A National Perspective

This paper draws on aspects of a national project looking at "Building Leadership Capacity in the Development and Sharing of Mathematics Learning Resources, Across Disciplines, Across Universities." The focus on building leadership capacity reflects the magnitude of the problem as beyond one person, and indeed one institution, and reflects the need for distributive leadership. From a leadership perspective there is a focus on recruiting others to engage others in the development and sharing or resources. If only it were that simple; the sharing of resources from a formal perspective involves varying intellectual property rights of institutions and copyright ownership by authors. Sharing within the bounds of the project involves tagging resources to show they are shared under a Creative Commons license [7], allowing the resource to be modified and used, provided the use is not-for-profit and attribution is given to the authors. A key strategy to engage other institutions has been to initiate participation in the project through two national symposia. Sharing in this project also involves housing and distributing quality assured resources so that teachers may control the use of those resources by embedding them in their course Web site. These are issues that continue to be addressed at an institutional and national level.

### 3.2 An Institutional Perspective

From an institutional and faculty perspective, the major issue becomes one of allocation of scarce resources to the development and housing of resources. The lead university on this project was keen to avoid duplication in the development of resources or in the exploration of approaches to improving teaching and learning outcomes using the created resources.

In the planning phases, preceding the national grant was a university request to scope the needs of faculties. This involved interviewing key stakeholders across the university campus. These included deans, heads of units, and individuals active in the development of support services and materials for students. It also involved mapping the failure rates in courses where mathematics and/or statistics were fundamental skills to identify the potential for making an impact in increasing passing grades.

In the operational phases of the project policies related to the purchase of nonstandard equipment, the Tablet PC became an issue, particularly for staff members whose desktops were managed from centralized IT services. Some staff members, in response to centralized management of computers, chose to use digital pens to create resources rather than Tablet PC technology, although Tablet PCs were the preferred and more flexible choice. The second major issue "under resolution" involves the housing of resources such that access to those resources is seamless in terms of integrating with Web-based learning management systems within institutions and at the same time allowing resources to be accessed and downloaded by those outside the host university. Again work is ongoing in resolving these issues.

### 3.3. Faculty, School, and Program Perspectives

At the faculty, school, and program levels the mapping of the need for resources remains broad. For the most part it is recognized that there are courses with a high level of mathematical content and that resources across topics in courses is required. Earlier work in our informatics faculty has indicated that while transitional resources for students are beneficial, resources for supporting students should be across all topics within courses, with priority in development afforded to the most difficult topics [3]. More detailed mapping of student needs is underway in our science faculty, where the need for students to translate science problems into mathematics problems and back to science has been identified as an issue.

### 3.4 Course Level Perspective

The work in developing resources typically takes place at a course level. At the course level, staff members have been able to map the problem topics and the misconceptions that need to be addressed in the resources. Here the sharing that has been of most value has been the sharing of expertise in the development of learning resources. Sharing has involved both technical support and creative inspiration as different functionalities have been explored and different genres of video have been developed. The sharing of expertise has transcended institutional boundaries. Sharing of resources across courses and institutions has begun, hampered at this stage by the as yet incomplete repository.

## 4. Evaluation

Evaluation of the project is multilayered. For our institution, evaluation is in terms of the sustainability of the learning support system and the effectiveness of that support system for students in courses dependent on mathematical skills.

The Tablet PC technologies have provided a mechanism for the sustainable development of learning resources. Early approaches to the development of videos involved the use of a camera mounted on a stand with subsequent addition of sound. This was followed by the use of a two-person video camera crew and subsequent editing. However, neither of these approaches was sustainable. The first approach was too difficult, while the second too costly in terms of time and money. It was only when Tablet PCs were introduced that the imagination of academic staff was captured, and they elected to develop their skills with Tablet PC technologies, including software such as PDF Annotator, Camtasia Studio, and PowerPoint, to create resources for their own students. Staff members have also begun to use Tablet PC technology creatively in class and importantly for the development of a learning support system, have begun to capture their teaching providing another source of materials that can be converted to support materials. There has been an uptake of the Tablet PC technology to create mathematics learning resources at a course level in nearly all of our disciplines—science, education, informatics, commerce, and engineering—with work also commencing in medicine. Lecturers have also begun to develop resources to support learning in their own disciplines. The community of practice that has developed in less than three years is self-sustainable without additional technical support required.

Evaluation in terms of improvement in student learning outcomes as a consequence of the video-based support resources has typically followed a research design that compares baseline evaluations of components of a course with evaluations by a new cohort after resources have been introduced. The most comprehensive evaluation has taken place for two cohorts of students in a first-year statistics course offered in 2009 and again in 2010 (n = 89 and n = 191) and a postgraduate introductory statistics course offered in 2008 and 2009 with students studying in distance mode (n = 20 and n = 14) and on-campus mode (n = 66 and n = 49). Evaluation has revealed that the use of the video clips (dominant method text questions with solutions written and spoken) created by Tablet PC in several courses has been associated with increased understanding and reduced student anxiety in learning statistics at both undergraduate and postgraduate levels [4]. Tablet PC-created video learning support resources were particularly popular with postgraduate students studying through a distance education mode [4]. While staff members seek to develop different genres to increase appeal, the dominant student commentary is simply "give us more."

## 5. Future Work

While the resources have been received favorably by students, one of the major questions currently being addressed is "How can student engagement with the learning resources be increased?" Addressing this question has led to exploration of learning designs. One of the typical mechanisms for including resources into e-learning environments is to gather all the resources for a one week segment of the course under one link (see Figure 1). An alternative is to create links that represent lectures, lab materials, data sets, assessment, and other key components of the course. A third approach is to combine both the weekly approach with the key components (see Figure 2).

**Figure 1.** Organization by week.

### GHMD983 STATISTICS FOR HEALTH RESEARCH

| Week 1 ⋎ | SubjectOutline 2009 ⋎ |
| Intro to Statistics | |
| Week 2 ⋎ | Assessment 2009 ⋎ |
| Exploratory techniques | |
| Week 3 ⋎ | Data 2008 ⋎ |
| Correlations | |
| Week 4 ⋎ | eduStream ⋎ |
| Regression | |
| Week 5 ⋎ | JMP Video support ⋎ |
| Probability | |

Learning designs in some contexts are represented as designs that can be documented in a systematic way, so that teachers can select, adapt, and use the design in their own teaching [2]. Several of our course coordinators are now trialing variants of a learning design model, the Learning Design Visual Sequence (LDVS) involving tasks, resources, and supports with accompanying documentation [1]. An example of this applied to an introductory statistics course is in Figure 3.

The map together with a statement of objectives has been used to represent the work students are to undertake and the resources that they can access. Evaluations of this work have yet to be completed.

**Figure 2.** Combined weekly materials and resource types.

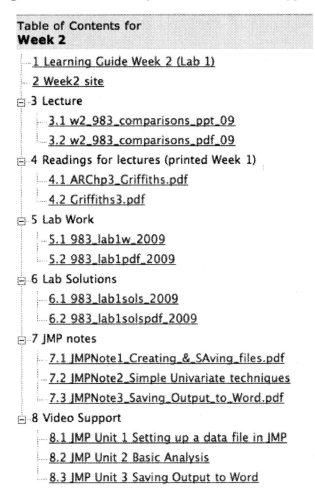

## 6. Conclusions

The work undertaken thus far has revealed the benefit of worked examples and more generally video clips for students learning in mathematics and statistics. The use of Tablet PC and associated technologies has been an integral component in the development of resources, allowing production to be taken into the hands of staff and students rather than remaining in the province of video crews. As such a sustainable approach to the development of resources for a learning support system has been obtained. However, in developing more resources we have become mindful of the need to produce optimal learning designs to engage students to use the support resources.

**Figure 3.** Learning Design Visual Sequence (LDVS) for one week's work in an introductory statistics course.

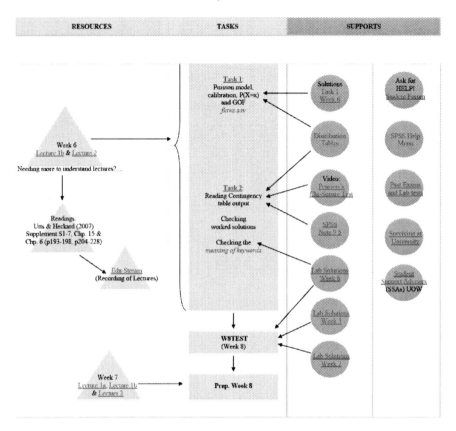

## 7. Acknowledgments

The authors gratefully acknowledge the important contributions and support provided for the production of this paper from the University of Wollongong and the Australian Learning and Teaching Council Ltd, an initiative of the Australian Government Department of Education, Employment and Workplace Relations. The views expressed in this paper do not necessarily reflect the views of the Australian Learning and Teaching Council Ltd.

## References

[1] Agostino, A.(2009). Learning Design representations to document, model and share teaching practice. In L. Lockyer, S. Bennett, S. Agostinho, and B. Harper (Eds). Handbook of Research on Learning design and Learning Objects: Issues, Applications and Technologies, 2009, 1-19. Information Science Reference.

[2] Agostinho, A., Bennett, S., Lockyer, L., Kosta, L., Jones, J., and Harper, B. An examination of learning design descriptions in an existing learning design repository. In *Same Places, Different Spaces*. Proceedings Ascillite, Auckland, 2009, 11-19. http://www.ascilite.org.au/conferences/auckland09/procs/agostinho.pdf.

[3] Aminifar, E., Porter, A. L., Caladine, R. J., and Nelson, M. I. Creating mathematical learning resources - combining audio and visual components. *ANZIAM Journal, 47* (2007) C934-C955.

[4] Baharun, N., and Porter, A. L. Teaching statistics using a blended approach: integrating technology-based resources. In *Same Places, Different Spaces*. Proceedings Ascillite, Auckland, 2009, 40-48.

[5] Barrington, F., and Brown, P. *Participation in Year 12 Mathematics Across Australia 1995-2004*. International Centre of Excellence for Education in Mathematics and the Australian Mathematical Sciences Institute, 2006. www.amsi.org.au/pdfs/Participation_in_Yr12_maths.pdf. Accessed 25 Mar. 2008.

[6] Clark, T, Nguyen, F, P., and Sweller, J. *Efficiency in Learning: Evidence-Based Guidelines to Manage Cognitive Load*. Pfeiffer, San Francisco, 2006.

[7] Creative Commons. http://www.creativecommons.org.au.

[8] Henderson, S., and P. Broadbridge. *Scoping project for Disciplines-Based Initiative Prog.* National Symposium, Mathematics for 21st Century Engineering Students, 2007. http://www.iru.edu.au/__data/assets/pdf_file/0020/180551/Phil-Broadbridge-AMSIs-perspective-on-the-national-curriculum.pdf.

[9] Wilson, T. *Maths & Stats learning support services in Australian Universities.* Report e-mailed to participants in the Quantitative diversity: disciplinary and cross-disciplinary mathematics and statistics support in Australian universities, July 2007.

# Student and Instructor Tablet PC Use Increases Retention in Undergraduate Mathematics Classes

*Carla A. Romney*

*Boston University*

## 1. Abstract

Undergraduate students often enter college with declared interests in one of the science, technology, engineering, or mathematics (STEM) fields, but they often switch their majors to non-STEM fields. Freshmen enroll in introductory mathematics courses to begin their formal STEM studies, but they quickly discover that these courses serve as gatekeepers to "weed out" students. Quantitative courses are often challenging for students because class time is devoted to lecture, and there are few opportunities to master the problem-solving techniques that are requisite for success. To address these limitations of conventional mathematics courses, we constructed a networked Tablet PC classroom that allows students to participate in interactive problem solving. The initial implementation occurred in College Algebra and Trigonometry (CAT), and students have progressed to Tablet PC offerings in Calculus I and II. Student attendance, retention, and performance were better in the Tablet PC enriched classes than in the same classes taught in non-Tablet PC settings. Tablet PCs are a promising pedagogical tool to improve mathematics instruction and concomitant retention in STEM.

## 2. Problem Statement and Context

A substantial number of undergraduate students indicate an interest in a STEM major when they apply to college and upon matriculation. Hurtado reported that approximately one-third of the 2009 Freshman Survey respondents indicated that they planned to pursue a STEM major, but other findings from this report are clarion calls for change in STEM education. In particular, their data show that less than half of the students who specify an interest in STEM upon college entry actually earn a STEM degree within five years. Even more troubling is their finding that students who initially entered undergraduate STEM programs had substantially lower degree completion rates (regardless of major selected) than their same-race peers who entered other academic disciplines [1]. While the reasons for poor retention during undergraduate education have not yet been determined, a possible explanation is that inadequate performance during the first year places students in academic jeopardy and leads them to alter their educational plans.

Introductory mathematics courses are gatekeepers that limit the number of students who pursue STEM degrees since many students do not earn passing grades in these classes and cannot continue their intended programs of study. Measurements that look only at recorded grades in introductory mathematics classes underestimate the magnitude of this problem. When students have difficulty in undergraduate mathematics classes, they often opt to drop or withdraw before grades appear on their transcripts rather than risk low grades. However, these students are forced to abandon their plans to enter quantitative disciplines and/or may choose to leave the institution entirely. Thus, mathematics courses present a unique opportunity to address the retention-to-degree problem because nearly every undergraduate student will enroll in a mathematics course. Improvements in mathematics classes that enhance student learning and performance may promote retention in STEM and in undergraduate degree programs.

One technological advance that has shown promise is the use of Tablet PCs in introductory mathematics courses. In non-Tablet PC secondary and undergraduate mathematics classes, students spend most of their class time copying information from the board or from an instructor's slides into a notebook rather than processing the information in a way that leads to knowledge and skill acquisition. Students in non-Tablet PC mathematics classes typically do not use computers for note-taking because it is cumbersome and time-consuming to use word processing equation editors to input the symbolic notation of mathematics. However, liberating students from their role as scribes can allow them to focus on understanding the material presented in class [2], and Tablet PCs are one way to promote this paradigm shift. Tablet PCs allow students to handwrite on the computer screen using a pen-like stylus, and their annotations ("inking") become part of their documents. When students have access to the bulk of the mathematics class content either before or during class, they can use Tablet PCs to actively annotate and clarify the information as it is presented rather than passively copying all of the material presented in class into their notebooks. Students can then engage in higher level thinking and concentrate on learning skills during class.

While the benefits of Tablet PCs for symbolic note-taking may argue for greater use of this technology in mathematics classes, there are other advantages that may emanate from their growing acceptance. For example, several software packages now facilitate bi-directional data transmission between networked Tablet PCs. This means that real-time interactive problem solving can take place in class as a means to solidify students' understanding of the content. Students can solve problems individually or in small groups, and their solutions can be displayed for analysis by the rest of the class or the instructor. Incorporating student work into the lecture not only serves to increase student engagement and participation, but also gives students opportunities to peer critique and learn from the various approaches used by their classmates. Networked Tablet PCs facilitate real-time formative evaluation of students' understanding and provide a means for instructors to recognize when they need to re-explain material that is difficult for students. These interventions can limit student frustration and may motivate students to work on the assigned homework.

Since there is a tremendous national need for a mathematically literate populace, we need to consider the deployment of new strategies to retain students who evince interest in fields that depend on mathematical understanding and problem-solving skills. Pedagogical innovations that couple Tablet PC technology with effective teaching may promote student retention in the quantitatively-based fields.

## 3. Solution Employed

A networked Tablet PC classroom provides an ideal means to minimize the difficulties faced by undergraduate students in introductory mathematics courses, so we sought to determine whether using these laptops would improve student engagement, performance, and retention. Tablet PCs address students' note-taking challenges since they abrogate the reliance on keyboarding as the primary method of data entry. Since the majority of the notes are provided by the instructor via PowerPoint slides that students view on the Tablet PCs, students do not need to focus on simply recording information. Students use the Tablet PC's stylus to take notes directly on the instructor's slides, and they save the edited versions of the files for subsequent review. This allows students to devote class time to thinking about the material that is presented and concentrate on learning how to use the information from class. Figure 1 is an instructor's ink annotated slide.

**Figure 1.** Instructor annotated PowerPoint slide.

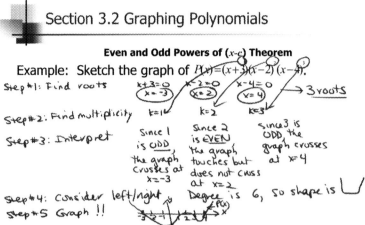

Hints:  Consider left/right behavior, *y*-intercept=*P*(0), *x*-intercept and crossing behavior, plot points, symmetry, etc.

Tablet PC technology also facilitates interactive problem solving and peer critiquing during lecture [2]. With networked Tablet PCs, students can transmit their work on problems to the instructor for display as part of a class discussion. Students can engage in peer-critiquing and learn from the mistakes and correct approaches used by their classmates. Students are more engaged in class when they are accountable for doing work during the session. The interactive problem solving and subsequent display of student work, which are possible with Tablet PCs, motivate students to remain on task since they do not know when their work will be displayed.

In order to evaluate the use of Tablet PCs in a series of Boston University undergraduate mathematics courses, a dedicated Tablet PC classroom was constructed with sixteen student Tablet PCs and one instructor Tablet PC that used the Microsoft Windows XP Tablet PC Edition 2005/Version 2002/Service Pack 3. Both Ethernet and wireless networking capabilities were used, and a LAN (local area network) was created. Classroom Presenter 3.0, a software package produced and freely distributed by the University of Washington, was used to permit real-time bi-directional data transfer between the instructor and students (http://classroompresenter.cs.washington.edu/). Classroom Presenter was selected as the backbone of this implementation because it enables the instructor to present the lectures and see all student-generated solutions that are submitted. The instructor can then select representative correct or incorrect responses to facilitate discussion and highlight important issues. Students obtained the instructor's PowerPoint slides at the beginning of class via a broadcast to all computers [3] through

Classroom Presenter, and they took notes during class by inking directly on the slides. Students were also given problems to solve during class, and they submitted their responses anonymously to the instructor using Classroom Presenter's submission capability. At the end of each class, they saved the PowerPoint slides (reformatted as .cp3 files by Classroom Presenter) with their notes on their own flash drives for review after class.

The instructor's Tablet PC was connected to an LCD projector to display the lecture slides. The instructor also simultaneously used Camtasia Studio 5.0 to produce videos that consisted of the instructor's annotated slides, all student work viewed in class, and completely synchronized audio that captured both the instructor and student comments. All lectures were converted to Adobe Shockwave/MP4 files, and they were posted on the CourseInfo or Blackboard (classroom management) site immediately after class. Students accessed the class recordings as desired.

The CAT course was selected for the initial implementation during fall 2008 since mastery of this course's content is often considered to be essential for students who intend to pursue STEM majors. This course is taken by first semester freshmen students who have indicated an interest in a quantitative discipline but who are deemed not to be ready to begin the calculus sequence without a rigorous review of the prerequisite mathematics content. As such, these students are most at risk for abandoning their pursuit of STEM majors. This course was selected for the Tablet PC intervention because it was likely that an effect on retention would be observable in this student population. In addition, the same instructor had taught comparably-sized non-Tablet PC enhanced sections of this course in fall 2005, 2006, and 2007 with the same textbook. Since the demographic profile of the undergraduate population at Boston University in general, and the eligible population for this class in particular, have not changed in any demonstrable way over this time period, we have a well matched reference population to study the impact of the Tablet PC-enhanced instruction.

## 4. Evaluation

Results from the first implementations of the Tablet PC-based interactive CAT classes in 2008 and 2009 indicate that the intervention has been beneficial. Student performance in the Tablet PC classes was better than performance in the comparable conventionally taught classes over the three prior years as illustrated in Figure 2.

**Figure 2.** Table of contents for MUSE online video textbook.

| YEAR | ENROLLMENT | WITHDRAWALS | < C- GRADES |
|---|---|---|---|
| 2008-2009 Tablet | 50 | 3 | 5 |
| 2005-2007 Non-Tablet | 56 | 5 | 8 |

While the numbers of students in these classes are still small, the significance of this preliminary finding is heightened because, unbeknownst to all students, the two in-class exams and the final exam were previously administered to the conventional "chalk talk" classes in 2005-2007. Since 80 percent of the final course grade was determined by the grades on these three examinations, there is moderate control for investigator bias in these results. Unlike examinations in other academic subjects, mathematics examinations are structured so that the answers can unequivocally be deemed correct or incorrect without succumbing to subjective assessments of student responses. This helps to reduce the likelihood that investigator-induced grade inflation as a self-fulfilling prophecy led to the improved performance.

In addition to the improvement in students' grades in the Tablet PC classes, student attendance in the Tablet PC classes was better than attendance in the conventionally taught control classes (99 percent in 2008-2009 vs. 96 percent in three prior years). Student retention in STEM after one semester was also greater for students in the Tablet PC classes than for their peers who took the comparable non-Tablet PC course (98 percent in 2008-2009 vs. 93 percent in three prior years). Retention in STEM is greater for students in the Tablet PC class than for students in the non-Tablet PC class (74 percent vs. 49 percent at the end of the first year, 63 percent vs. 33 percent at the end of the second year).

One concern that emerged during the development of the Tablet PC classroom was whether students would simply stop attending class because the class recordings would be readily available immediately after class on the class Web site. As shown in Figure 3, the number of Web site hits per student during the semester increased dramatically with the introduction of the Tablet PCs.

However, the number of hits per student does not reveal what students were doing when they used the Web site. An analysis of the Web site utilization pattern revealed a switch from using the Web site primarily to access the homework solutions to using the Web site for the class recordings. Interestingly, students did not use the Web site in lieu of attending class since attendance was slightly higher in the Tablet PC class than in the comparable non-Tablet PC classes.

Another important observation from this study is that the introduction of the Tablet PC did not change the instructor's student evaluations. The evaluation of

**Figure 3.** Web site utilization data for Tablet PC and non-Tablet PC classes.

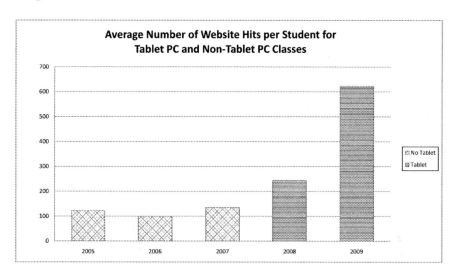

the course was not significantly changed (score of 4.66 out of 5 in the Tablet PC classes vs. 4.83 out of 5 in the non-Tablet PC classes). Many instructors resist introducing technology such as Tablet PCs into their classes because they fear that their evaluations may suffer if their students do not embrace the pedagogical innovation. Nevertheless, this risk must be balanced by the benefits that may accrue to students if the implementation is well executed.

## 5. Future Work

During spring 2009, the students who participated in the fall 2008 CAT class continued their study of mathematics by taking Calculus I with another instructor who also used the Tablet PCs in the same interactive classroom environment. To complete the undergraduate mathematics core courses, Tablet PC-based Calculus II was offered to these students in fall 2009. Ultimately, we want to determine whether this intervention has a positive effect on student retention in mathematics and STEM fields.

Finally, the Tablet PC interactive classroom technology can be used not only in face-to-face instruction, but also in online and distance education, growing segments of the higher education marketplace. During fall 2008, one student traveled extensively and was unable to attend some class sessions in person. We successfully demonstrated the use of Web-conferencing software coupled with Classroom Presenter so that students can participate in the class from remote sites. We expect that this will be an area of growth for Tablet PC-based instruction.

# References

[1] Hurtado, S., Eagen, K., and Chang, M. Research Brief: *Degrees of Success: Bachelor's Degree Completion Rates among Initial STEM Majors* Higher Education Research Institute (HERI) at UCLA, Los Angeles, CA, 2010, 1-4. http://heri.ucla.edu/nih/HERI_ResearchBrief_OL_2010_STEM.pdf. Accessed June 7, 2010.

[2] Huettel, L. G., Forbes, J., Franzoni, L., Malkin, R., Nadeau, J., and Ybarra, G. Using tablet PCs to enhance engineering and computer science education. *The Impact of Tablet PCs and Pen-based Technology on Education: Beyond the Tipping Point.* J. C. Prey, et al. (Eds.). Purdue University Press, 2007, 59-66.

[3] Anderson, R., Anderson, R., McDowell, L., and Simon, B. Use of Classroom Presenter in engineering courses. *Proceedings of the 35th ASEE/IEEE Frontiers in Education Conference*, 2005.

# Building a Better Math Tutor System with Tablet PC Technology

*Aaron Wangberg, Nicole Anderson, Chris Malone,*
*Beya Adamu, Kristin Bertram, and Katherine Uber*

*Winona State University*

## 1. Abstract

College calculus requires students to apply knowledge and reasoning about pre-calculus concepts to new problems. Students who struggle to recall precalculus material, or rely upon memorization of those techniques, have trouble succeeding in calculus. This paper reports how some instructors in the Department of Mathematics at Winona State University have utilized Session, a Web-based interactive digital ink tutorial program, and WeBWorK, an open-source online homework system, to help struggling calculus students understand prerequisite material. We show how digital ink better engages students in the solution to mathematics problems than text-based solutions, and how question prompts, based upon self-explanation guidelines, help students understand the solution's steps. Pre/posttest and course grades show less prepared calculus students interacted with the tutorials more frequently than unsuccessful calculus students. We also compare student perceptions of the effectiveness of the tutorials with a control group of students who viewed static online solutions to mathematics problems. Finally, we report modifications that will help students more fully utilize the interactive tutorials.

## 2. Problem Statement and Context

Correct recall and understanding of precalculus material can help students succeed in calculus. In fall 2008, the average initial assessment score on precalculus material for 150 college calculus students at Winona State University was 50.7 percent, as measured by commercial online testing software. After a review period of six weeks, successful (A/B/C) students in the course improved their score by 20 percentage points, while unsuccessful (D/F/W) students improved 13 percentage points. During this review period, students sought help from both the commercial testing software, which provided an online textbook and glossary of mathematics terms, and from peer student tutors in the department-run Mathematics Achievement Center (MAC). Post-course data shows that successful calculus students spent 45 percent more time in the MAC during the review period than unsuccessful students.

**Figure 1.** Digital ink provides a fast way to write mathematics in session. Users can write solutions without knowing LaTeX or other mathematical typesetting languages.

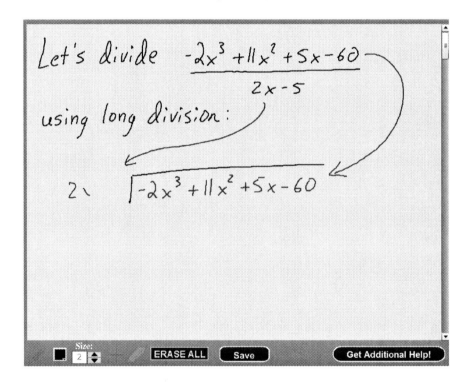

Although less convenient and more costly, success was higher when students worked with MAC tutors than with the static online text. MAC tutors work on whiteboards and help struggling students understand an answer by asking them to explain the solution's difficult steps in their own words. The students were practicing a form of self-explanation, a technique shown by several cognitive scientists to lead to better learning [1, 2, 3, 5]. Cognitive scientists have found that expert learners are more likely than novice learners to use the technique, and the tutor interactions helped struggling students spend more time on difficult material. During the fall 2008 study, students reported being more engaged in the MAC with tutors than with the online text. This engagement with tutors in self-explanation techniques could have influenced why students were more successful when working with MAC tutors than with the online text.

## 3. Solution Employed

The challenge of this project was to design an online tutorial system that could imitate the MAC tutor/student interactions and improve test scores on prerequisite material. In the MAC, tutors and students scattered quick graphs and calculations on whiteboard-covered tables. Tutors handed students markers and encouraged them to finish partially-worked problems. Tutors also interrupted students, pointed to part of their work, and asked them to explain various steps. The new tutorial system needed to facilitate all of these actions in an online environment. These interactions required digital ink.

In 2008, the first author created interactive online tutorial software, called Session, which uses digital ink to programmatically replicate many of the interactions that occurred between calculus students and human tutors in the MAC. Built on code available from [4], Session is a Flash-based applet designed as a digital whiteboard, which records the time and location of a user's pen as they write with digital ink. Stored in a MySQL database, this digital ink can be replayed instantly or in "scaled real-time" for other users.[1] This system can show students how an expert would solve a mathematics problem, as shown in Figures 1, 2, and 3. This system is especially helpful for solutions in which steps are not written left-to-right and top-to-bottom.

Digital ink allows instructors to create mathematics tutorials incorporating self-explanation techniques in minutes with the Session software. To create a tutorial, the instructor begins writing the solution to a mathematics problem on the Session whiteboard with digital ink. The instructor can pause their writing and insert a question for the student at any time in writing the solution; six different question types (free-response, multiple-choice, true/false, checkbox, draw, and graph) are available. Questions can be placed within the Session whiteboard area, as indicated in Figure 4, or in a standard framed box below the whiteboard, as shown in Figure 5. The Session software supports self-explanation practices by allowing the instructor to ask the student to provide both an answer and a reason for their answer to a question. The instructor provides their own "expert" answer and reason, as shown in Figure 5, allowing students to check and/or correct their own thinking. After asking a question, the instructor continues writing their solution to the problem. Although most contain three or four, tutorials can use any number of student questions.

**Figure 2.** Session acts like a digital whiteboard. Users can adjust pen color and size, erase ink, type, and incorporate graphs and images into their session.

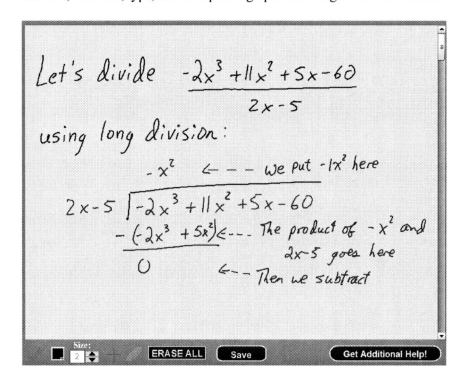

**Figure 3.** Session replays an instructor's solution to a math problem and the students see the steps occur in scaled real-time,1 approximately one-third the time required to write the solution with digital ink.

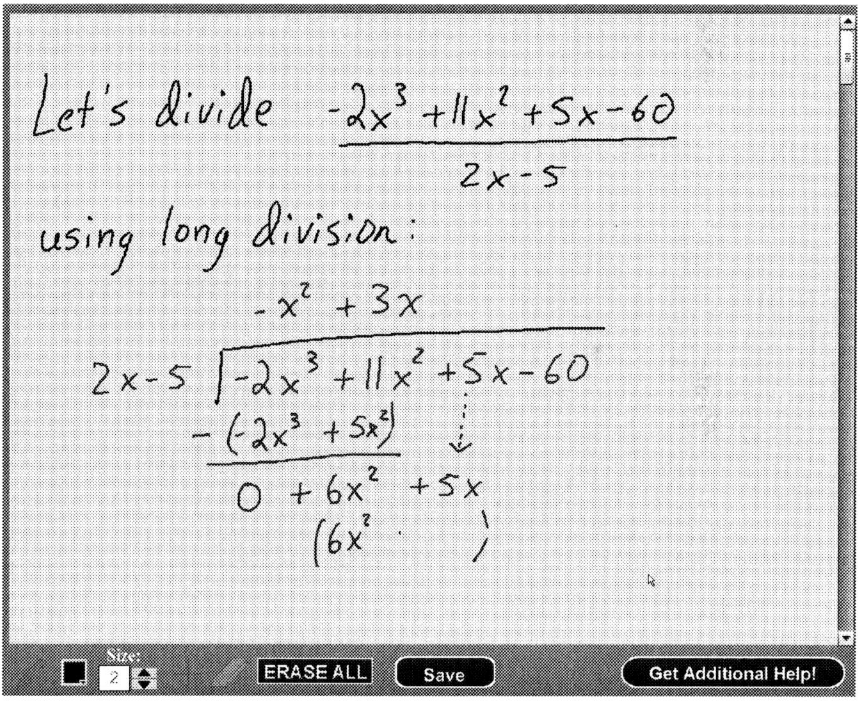

**Figure 4.** Questions placed within the Session tutorial help students focus on specific mathematical steps.

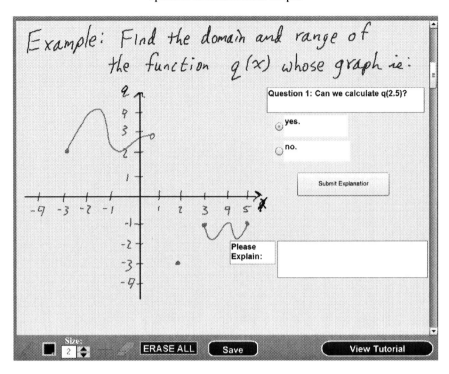

WeBWorK, an open-source online mathematics homework system, was modified to deliver the appropriate tutorial to struggling students. Students were given a pretest in WeBWorK consisting of eighty-four different precalculus questions with each question pulled from a different precalculus Concept Bank. Individual students were assigned three practice problems from the associated Concept Bank for each incorrect pretest question. The WeBWorK online interface was modified to seamlessly incorporate the Session software. In this interface, the Session software could provide an online whiteboard space where students could solve the corresponding WeBWorK problem, as shown in Figure 6, or it could show the tutorial corresponding to the WeBWorK problem. Together, WeBWorK and Session recorded student performance data (number of correct or incorrect attempts) as well as data about student behaviors (amount of time spent viewing and interacting with the tutorials).

## 4. Evaluation

One section of calculus students (n = 43) used the Session/WeBWorK system during the spring 2010 semester at Winona State University. Tutorials were written for thirty-two of the eighty-four precalculus Concept Banks. A student was automatically shown a tutorial after their third incorrect answer to problems from one of these Concept Banks. For comparison purposes, students in a similar, but separate, section (n = 45) of calculus reviewed precalculus material using a commercial system that incorporated worked examples shown on static Web pages. Students using the commercial software could view a worked problem at any time but were forced to view the solution after their third wrong attempt at a practice problem. Both systems assigned practice problems and posttest questions for individual students based upon their pretest performance. The two systems provided quantitative data, which is summarized below. Student surveys provided qualitative data on the effectiveness of the Session tutorial implementation.

**Figure 5.** Placing questions below the Session tutorial guides students away from specific steps and toward analyzing overall procedures.

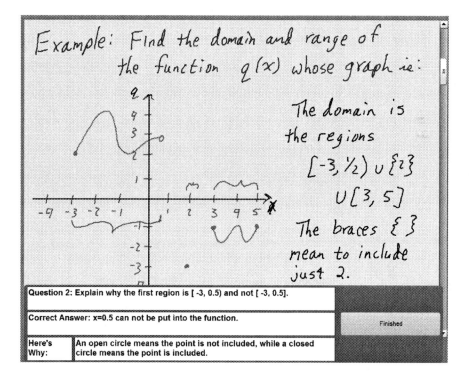

**Figure 6.** Embedded into the WeBWorK interface, the Session software can both show a student a relevant tutorial and save their solution, as shown above.

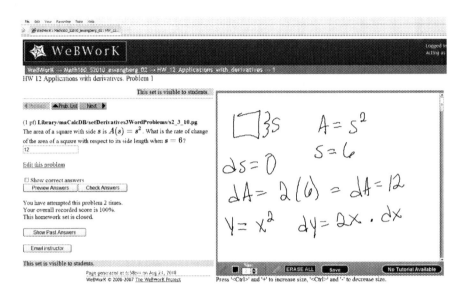

### 4.1 Effect of Tutorials on Student Learning

Tutorials were shown to 43 students struggling with particular precalculus concepts, but only 17 students used this interactive help. Excluding the ignored tutorials, slightly more than half (31) of the 52 tutorials shown were watched in full. Students who viewed a tutorial in full measured more improvement (62 percent) than those who viewed only part of a tutorial (53 percent). Designed to help students understand, not memorize, solutions to mathematics problems, the Session tutorials were particularly helpful for students scoring in the lowest quartile on the pretest. As measured by WeBWorK and the Session software, these students spent more time (2.22 hours) working with the system than unsuccessful (D/F/W) students (1.6 hours). On average, they spent more time working with the tutorials (2.3 minutes) than "C" students (1.96 minutes), but significantly less than either "A" or "B" students (10.1 and 7.6 minutes, respectively). Every D/F/W student with an initial pre-score above the bottom quartile ignored the tutorials.

An analysis of covariance approach was used to compare the performance of calculus students using the WeBWorK/Session system to those using the commercial system. Figure 7 shows the influence of each system on the rate of improvement. The slope of the regression line for the WeBWorK/Session system is slightly higher suggesting a higher rate of improvement. The trends in Figure

7 were similar when investigating the final exam performance of students in both courses.

**Figure 7.** Posttest versus pretest scores for the two systems. Students scoring above 34.7 percent on the pretest showed more improvement when using WeBWorK/Session than when using the commercial system.

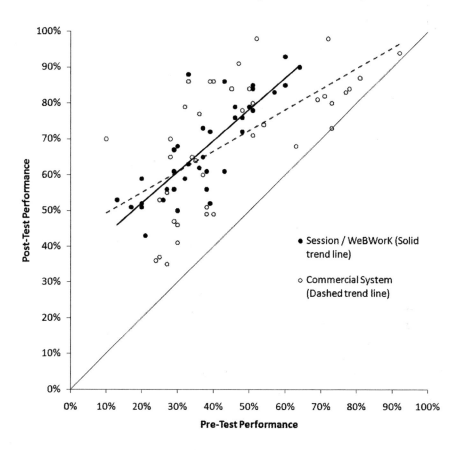

It was not possible to track the amount of interaction students had with the commercial system's static worked examples. However, both pretest score and the total number of hours spent with the system statistically influence the posttest scores in each system. After adjusting for a student's pretest score and total hours, the expected posttest score for a student using the commercial system is statistically lower than the WeBWorK/Session system (p-value = 0.0123). The posttest score is expected to be about 5 percent lower for the commercial system.

## 4.2 Implementation Evaluation

Students from both calculus sections were given a survey asking about their experience reviewing precalculus content with their respective system. A high percentage of students (88.9 percent) found the worked examples in the commercial system helpful, although 75 percent of the students indicated there were occasional steps they could not explain in these solutions. Comparatively, 42.9 percent of the students found the tutorials helpful in the Session/WeBWorK system.

Three implementation issues contributed to lower satisfaction ratings for Session tutorials:

- The Session software scaled according to screen size, making tutorial prompts difficult to read. Students comprising 57.3 percent reported the tutorials were difficult to read or use.

- The replay rate was fixed at 36 percent of the time it took to write the tutorial. Although 61.1 percent of the students found the replay rate appropriate, nearly half (38.9 percent) of the students thought the replay rate was too slow. No one reported it was too fast.

- Tutorials only existed for 32 of the 84 different precalculus Concept Banks, limiting the number of opportunities students had to interact with tutorials. Nearly all (91.7 percent) of the students wanted the option to view relevant tutorials.

Asked their preference of a single change in the implementation model, most students wanted more opportunities to view tutorials. Half (50.6 percent) of the students preferred to view all the tutorials, and 23.4 percent of the students wanted the option to see the tutorial more than once. We initially assumed students who answered a question correctly would not need to see the tutorial, but 19.5 percent of the students would have preferred this option. Only 3.9 percent of the students wanted to make more attempts at the problems before the tutorial appeared.

## 4.3 Tutorial Interaction Evaluation

The difference between a correct answer to a mathematical problem and an incorrect answer can often hinge on a student's understanding of one or two key steps in the solution. The design of the self-explanation tutorials forced students to think about the difficult parts of the math problems. This active learning can be frustrating for the student, but nearly half (48.6 percent) of the students reported that this helped them understand the related concept. Students also had the option of viewing an expert's explanations for those steps, and 77.8 percent of the students found these explanations helpful.

Interestingly, most students (69.4 percent) working with the commercial system thought it would be beneficial to be able to view a relevant interactive tutorial for practice problems.

## 5. Future Work

A number of improvements will be made to the Session/WeBWorK system to help students interact with the tutorials. Tutorials will be added for the other precalculus Concept Banks, and struggling students will be able to immediately select a tutorial from a few relevant options. The system will provide a message about the instructor's office hours or MAC tutor hours to students continuing to struggle with problems. Finally, students will be able to "peek" at another student's solution written with digital ink and analyze it using preset tutorial questions.

## 7. Acknowledgments

This work was made possible through a Center for Teaching and Learning grant with funding from the Office of the Chancellor, Minnesota State Colleges and Universities. The Dean of the College of Science and Engineering at Winona State University provided additional funding.

## Notes

1    Our tutorials replay digital ink in 36 percent of the time it took an instructor to write a problem.

## References

[1] Aleven, V., and Koedinger, K. R. An effective meta-cognitive strategy: learning by doing and explaining with a computer-based Cognitive Tutor. *Cognitive Science*, 26, 2 (2002) 147-179.

[2] Bielaczyc, K., Pirolli, P. and Brown, A. L. Training in Self-Explanation and Self-Regulation Strategies: Investigating the Effects of Knowledge Acquisition Activities on Problem Solving. *Cognition and Instruction,* 13 (1995) 221-252.

[3] Chi, M. T. H. Self-explaining expository texts: The dual processes of generating inferences and repairing mental models. In R. Glaser (Ed.), *Advances in instructional psychology*. Lawrence Erbaum Associates, Mahwah, NJ, 2000, 161-238.

[4] Ensley, D., and Kaskocz, B. *Drawing with the mouse example*. http://www.flashandmath.com/basic/mousedraw/index.html. 2004.

[5] Renkl, A. Learning mathematics from worked-out examples: Analyzing and fostering self-explanations. *European Journal of Psychology of Education, 14 (1999)* 477-488.

# PART TWO

# Abstracts

# Learning *by* numbers: Large scale peer-to-peer learning with Monash MeTL

*Nathan Bailey, Katharina Franke, Chris Hagan, David Hagan, and Murray Logan*

*Monash University*

Monash University has been exploring Tablet PC-based education since 2008. An integral part has been the use of Classroom Presenter (CP). When both students and instructors have access to Tablet PCs, CP provides opportunities for increased interaction, participation, and instant feedback. Our findings indicate that students perceive Tablet PC-based teaching as more engaging and interactive than non-Tablet PC-based classes.

However, interaction with CP remains largely focused on instructor-student feedback, limiting the power of collaboration and peer-based instruction that can significantly enhance engagement and learning. To address this, Monash started to develop its own software, Monash MeTL, allowing us to progressively move toward a collaborative approach where students can work together with peers and the instructor in exploring the lecture topic.

Currently, Monash MeTL incorporates a number of common interactive features, including importing PowerPoint slides for annotation, adding whiteboard space, and creating structured quizzes. MeTL's full potential is best realized when students take advantage of the shared visual space to collaborate as part of the classroom experience and beyond. Since MeTL is server-persistent, students and instructors have access to MeTL anytime, anywhere, enabling them to collaborate and continue their learning experience beyond the classroom.

In 2010, MeTL (2.0) was used in two Medicine cohorts, allowing students to interact with peers during class and to collaboratively construct their understanding of the lecture content. Rigorous testing took place in early 2010 to prepare for the rollout, which indicates that MeTL is able to host about nine hundred simultaneous participants per server.

# Creativity Unleashed: Digital Ink "Erases" Constraints and Allows Teachers to Focus on Pedagogy

## *Robert Baker*

*Cincinnati Country Day School*

Tablet PCs are paradigm-shifting educational tools that have allowed Cincinnati Country Day School to integrate technology as we had dreamed of doing when we first began our laptop program in 1996. These swiveling wonders give teachers the freedom and flexibility to reach beyond the machine and focus on student learning.

A Tablet PC 1:1 environment is not evolutionary; it is revolutionary in comparison to a standard laptop deployment. In a non-Tablet PC deployment, so much energy is expended trying to fit the tools to the task. Digital ink allows one to achieve the lofty goals of seamless collaboration, transparent technology integration, and personalized instruction. Tablet PCs allow equations and drawings to be used in collaborative and engaging ways, but without the constraints of time and space. The humanities can also take advantage of digital ink, whether by diagramming sentences, offering inked up feedback on student essays, or creating the next great work of art.

Ongoing formative assessment is essential to the learning process. A Tablet PC environment provides the instructor with a window into a student's work, notes, drawings, and process, with near instantaneity. Perhaps this glimpse into a child's methods of essay writing happens while they are at home at night, struggling with thesis development; perhaps it takes place in class while they are solving quadratic equations or graphing parabolas. Because the work is in digital form, written with a stylus, the instructors are better equipped to take the pulse of a class and offer feedback in natural and immediate ways.

# Using Conceptual Maps to Support Instructors in Designing Tablet PC-based Courses

*José-V. Benlloch-Dualde, Félix Buendía,*
*Juan-Carlos Cano, and Lenin Lemus Zúñiga*

*Universidad Politécnica de Valencia*

Although there is an extensive literature describing Tablet PC-based courses at different education levels, it is not easy to find publications that describe how to support instructors in designing such courses.

As the possibilities for Tablet PCs grow, it seems appropriate to address the conceptualization of these technologies from an instructional point of view. Among the different tools for organizing and representing knowledge, we have decided to use conceptual maps. We introduce such structures to model both the instructional requirements in a specific educational setting as well as the potential Tablet PC uses. The main goal in processing these conceptual maps is to look for relationships that ultimately can provide instructors with some guidelines for designing Tablet PC-based courses.

In order to test this approach, a four-hour workshop has been designed. Instructors attending the workshop are invited to answer a pre-workshop questionnaire in order to easily obtain their learning requirements. In fact, the questions presented to the faculty are connected to the concepts and relationships of a rather general instructional map. Then, the instructional possibilities related to Tablet PC technologies are presented in a very hands-on way. Finally, a post-workshop questionnaire focused on the technology domain is presented. This allows us to look at the relationships between the two domains.

Even though the approach is still under development, initial results seem promising as a way to help instructors design Tablet PC-based courses.

# Scaling a Grassroots Tablet PC Pilot for Large-Scale Campus Integration

*Dave A. Berque, Terri L. Bonebright, and Carol L. Smith*

*DePauw University*

We discuss a strategy for expanding a successful Tablet PC teaching initiative from a small pilot to a more broadly-based campus initiative. DePauw University received Hewlett-Packard Technology for Teaching Grants in 2006 and 2007. The grants supported the redesign of three courses to use in-class group problem solving, collaborative note-taking, and other active-learning activities enabled by the Tablet PCs and DyKnow software. The grant activities included a formal mixed-method assessment that combined (a) a formal experimental study of the impact of Tablet PCs on collaborative problem solving and (b) an ecologically valid classroom study.

We partnered with University faculty development programs to present the grant activities and our assessment findings across campus through a variety of hands-on workshops and presentations. We also partnered with the Admission Office to offer pen-based computing "mock classes" for prospective students visiting campus, and with the Alumni Office during reunion weekend to engage members of the 50th reunion class in a mock class. These events helped us to broaden campus interest in our project. While our original plans called for a handful of course redesigns, interest in the project has resulted in the use of the equipment in 77 courses enrolling more than 1,200 students in 11 disciplines. Funds provided by the academic vice president allowed us to loan additional Tablet PCs to faculty members for use in teaching and research. The success of these pilots led to the addition of a Tablet PC option to our existing 1:1 computing programs for both students and faculty.

# Reading and Note-taking on Tablet PCs versus Paper: A Comparative Pilot Study

## Craig Leonard Brians and Chelsea Aleena Hickey

### Virginia Polytechnic and State University

As digital media replace paper for academic reading, students may need to develop new skills to comprehend and retain this digital information. College students typically use computers on a daily basis in their social and educational lives. However, few systematic studies have been performed on the comprehension and retention of digital scholarly information, and the results of the existing research have been equivocal. Some research finds advantages with learning from digital media (Kozma 1991; Chen et al. 2007), paper sources show greater information retention in others (Dillon 1992), while other studies fail to find a difference (Clark 2001; Doolittle and Chambers 2004).

In this study we plan to test a new theory of information retention from digital versus paper sources, focusing on the benefits of pen-based computing. Specifically, this study models the relative advantages of writing notes on a paper document versus writing notes on a digital document. Additionally, we will control for users' reading preferences.

We expect to find that students who prefer to read on paper more accurately comprehend and retain both digital and paper information. Using the pen-based computing interface to take notes is expected to reduce the retention gap between paper and digital information sources. Although this pilot study will involve fewer than fifty subjects, it should demonstrate the value of pursuing further research on the educational implications of reading digital versus paper media.

# Using Pen-based Technology to Improve Instruction in Engineering Economics

*Glen P. Ciborowski and Bruce V. Mutter*

*Bluefield State College*

CART, Inc. worked with the School of Engineering Technology and Computer Science (SET) at Bluefield State College (BSC) to implement a more active learning environment for teaching a junior-level engineering economics course (ENGR 315). Using a pen-based Tablet PC coupled with the CART CMS, a Moodle-based course management service and interactive software, our instructional approach was modified to convert the traditional lecture-based ENGR 315 course to a more student-centered live learning environment. This method is now being planned for introductory mathematics and advanced computer science courses. Results show that the use of pen-based Tablet PC coupled with live capture of the lecture posted on the CART CMS have resulted in better student retention and improved attention during the course. There is evidence of improved student performance and faculty evaluations.

Using the Tablet PC instead of whiteboards, overheads, and blackboards allowed the ENGR 315 instructor to: (1) face students naturally and continually while solving equations; (2) produce cash flow diagrams more accurately and efficiently; (3) eliminate interruptions and distractions caused by physical transitions between whiteboard and projector screen; (4) quickly introduce color during live presentations that further improve understanding of concepts and classroom discussions; (5) facilitate student note-taking through CART CMS posts that improve organization and elaboration; (6) accommodate student review for tests and quizzes; (7) provide students with a ready-made, savable, printable, portfolio useful for Fundamentals of Engineering (FE) review and exam preparation; and (8) work more high-quality problem examples due to these increased course delivery efficiencies.

# Tablet Computing as Enablement for Personalized Learning Communities in High School and College Mathematics Classrooms

*Eric Hamilton, Brian Fisher, and Kevin Iga*

*Pepperdine University*

This effort, funded by Microsoft Research, the U.S. Air Force Academy, and Pepperdine University, advances a vision for personalized learning communities in mathematics education. The advent of network communication tools that allow teachers to view student work in thumbnail and full screen form, coupled with Tablet PCs permitting freehand mathematical notation, permits a new form of classroom dynamics that emphasizes salutary aspects of both individualization and community within the classroom, in an effort to solve the need to elevate mathematical engagement by students. One lens for analyzing classroom dynamics involves the construct of interactional bandwidth, which refers to the quantity of personal and content interaction that can pass over the classroom communication systems. (One way to describe bandwidth involves the use of a classroom response system [CRS]. A classroom that adds a CRS also adds bandwidth, another avenue for important information to cross hands. The same can be said for any configuration that furnishes electronic communication between members of the classroom.) The solution we employ to elevate engagement with Tablet PCs entails significantly multiplying the interactional bandwidth of a classroom, allowing the teacher and the students to co-navigate large bodies of visual data that a) disclose student mathematical thinking in richer detail; b) enable more timely and richly informed feedback by the teacher to the student; and c) sustain significantly higher levels of mathematical engagement in the classroom. The pen-based computing solution entailed furnishing every pair of students with one Tablet PC, using Windows Journal and collaboration software.

# Diffusion of the Tablet PC through the College of Engineering at Virginia Tech

*Shreya Kothaneth, Catherine Amelink,*
*and Glenda Scales*

*Virginia Polytechnic and State University*

The College of Engineering (COE) at Virginia Polytechnic and State University is considered a vanguard with using new technology to enrich the teaching and learning experience. In 2006, the COE started the Tablet PC initiative, which required all incoming engineering freshman students to purchase a Tablet PC. The Department of Engineering Education (ENGE) is the first introduction for engineering students to the educational environment within the college as all incoming freshmen are required to take two introductory courses offered by ENGE. A qualitative investigation revealed that ENGE faculty members not only readily adopted the Tablet PC, but have also helped faculty members outside of their department learn how to effectively use the technology. Some of the Department's faculty members are also considered to be champions of various technologies. Interestingly enough, COE has found it challenging to get other departments to accept the Tablet PC as readily as ENGE. A thirty-minute focus group was conducted in order to understand what motivated the faculty members of ENGE to adopt the Tablet PC. The analysis based on Everett Rogers' Diffusion of Innovations Theory found a correlation between Rogers' attributes, user profiles, and the successful innovation-adoption profile. Thus, we suggest that in order to successfully diffuse an innovation, one must try and increase the relative advantage, compatibility, observability, trialability, and reduce the complexity of a technology. Also, we believe that champions play an important role in the diffusion of a product. Through this work, we hope to help encourage adoption of the Tablet PC.

# Microsoft Shared OneNote in a 1:1 Fifth through Twelfth Grade Environment: A Collaboration and Workflow Utopia

## *Gregory K. Martin*

### *Cincinnati Country Day School*

At Cincinnati Country Day School educators use OneNote in a shared environment, allowing teachers to do more and better formative assessment by having a window into student work anytime and anywhere. Students in courses as far ranging as fifth grade French and upper school physics are able to continue to work within the paper notebook paradigm, but with greater multimedia and collaborative capabilities. Students place everything from handwritten notes to audio/video clips in a notebook that can be shared with the classroom teacher and/or other students in the class, thus leading to more effective collaboration. The goal at Cincinnati Country Day School was to create a school-wide environment in which the sharing of information was simple, effective, flexible, and enabled both creativity and productivity. OneNote enabled us to do this in several ways. For instance, it enables digital portfolio capabilities like no other form of technology. Clearly applicable in language arts courses, the model can transfer to other disciplines as well. OneNote can also be used as a means of disseminating handouts, worksheets, and writing prompts that students can ink up or type on. Teachers can then navigate through all students' work in a timely and efficient manner.

# SuperIDR: A Tablet PC Tool for Image Description and Retrieval

*Uma Murthy,[1] Nadia P. Kozievitch,[2] Edward A. Fox,[1] Ricardo Torres,[2] and Eric Hallerman[1]*

*[1]Virginia Polytechnic and State University and [2]University of Campinas*

SuperIDR is a Tablet PC-based tool that combines text and visual content-based image description and retrieval. It allows users to mark parts of images and associate them with text annotations. Annotations can be entered using either pen-based or keypad-based input. Later, users can browse information and perform text- and content-based search on textual descriptions, annotations, images, and parts of images. We developed SuperIDR as an aid to fish species identification and seeded it with images and descriptions of freshwater fishes of Virginia. We evaluated SuperIDR in an ichthyology class at Virginia Tech (VT) and found that students had a higher likelihood of success with SuperIDR than with traditional methods for species identification. Later, we adapted SuperIDR to work with parasite images and descriptions for zooparasitology students at UNICAMP, Brazil. In two studies at UNICAMP, students tested SuperIDR and felt that it was useful for species identification. In all studies (VT and UNICAMP), students had some difficulty with pen-based input and felt that they needed more training to use it effectively. Overall, we found that students (and teachers) had a positive reaction to SuperIDR as an aid to species identification. A new version of Super-IDR (to be made available for download) will include combined text and image search as well as the ability to compare two images side by side, while marking and annotating them. Also, we will conduct a qualitative study to understand the use of SuperIDR in the workplace and field. We hope to get more subjective and detailed feedback from this study.

# Designing a Web-based System
# for Tagging Errors in Freshman Calculus
# Using Pen-based Technology

*Roy P. Pargas, Eric Anderson, Marilyn Reba,*
*and Calvin Williams*

*Clemson University*

Pen-based technology motivated the construction of a large database of student work in calculus, both inked and scanned, through which the tagging and analysis of student errors and problem-solving strategies becomes possible. To minimize failure rates, we want to know where students in at-risk groups, and students in general, are making errors and then, guided by an extensive statistical error analysis, develop and evaluate new teaching materials and online instructional interventions. Due to collaboration between the Department of Mathematical Sciences and the Department of Computer Science, funded both by Hewlett-Packard and the National Science Foundation, we have been able to enhance the Web-based software, MessageGrid, to meet the needs of this tagging project. The process of developing an error-analysis study based on tagging involves the interplay of four components: (a) student-inked submissions; (b) item-analysis statistics; (c) a tagging lexicon; and (d) Web-based software. In summer 2010, several faculty members and graduate students developed a lexicon of errors and tagged over two thousand Calculus I finals from fall 2009.

# Patient Problem Posing (3P)

## *Kevin J. Reins*

*The University of South Dakota*

Students often become impatient when they are not readily able to resolve diffi-cult mathematical problems. The author's experimentation with "patient problem posing" in Ubiquitous Presenter (UP) demonstrated positive effects on students' perceptions of problem solving. This technique requires little setup time for an instructor to deploy, can be used as in-class experiences or activities occurring outside of class time, evokes and encourages students' intuitions, and allows op-portunities to build a problem and its resolution.

Five steps describe patient problem posing: (1) create and upload a Power-Point slide that poses a significant problem with deep structure to UP; (2) estab-lish an aura of excitement and enable student slide submissions; (3) be *patient* and allow students necessary time for struggle, problem-solving, and entering solutions; (4) critique and review the student submitted slides by syncing with the UP lecture; and (5) help students extract lessons from the UP experience by engaging them in analytic and evaluative reflection.

It was found that this environment allowed students to apply their own frameworks and see connectedness and generalizations within mathematics. Stu-dents were better able to evaluate the status of an algorithm or idea, its (a) *intel-ligibility*, knowing what it means and being able to represent the conception, (b) *plausibility*, believing it to be true and that it is consistent with other conceptions within one's schema, and (c) *fruitfulness*, it achieves something of value and solves an insoluble problem or serves as a powerful means of interpreting other phenomena, while sense making.

# Student Help Desk Support for Tablet PC and Pen-based Computing Environment

*Kevin Rokuskie*

*Cary Academy*

How can a school district or private school handle the hardware, software, and numerous other requests that are associated with a Tablet PC and pen-based computing 1:1 computer environment? It all starts with the information technology staff and the support model that they put in place. If the support is not available for faculty, staff, and students, then frustration can mount, which means people may not use the Tablet PC for its intended purpose. Even if the information technology support staff is available, they might not be able to handle all requests. How can this support be supplemented and added to the classroom? Utilizing a student help desk is a great benefit for the school to use with a Tablet PC and pen-based computing environment. Cary Academy has used a student help desk environment since the school began using Tablet PCs in the fall of 2006. The class is called CANE (Computer and Network Essentials). Upper school students take this as an extra class and come to the Information Technology Support Office located in the middle school, during a study hall, free period, or after school. Students learn the basics of hardware and software troubleshooting, networking, and minor repairs. This can eventually lead to a summer internship with the Information Technology staff, which includes a résumé and interview process. Learn how to utilize the best resource you have—the students who use the Tablet PCs and other pen-based computers.

# Pen-based Technologies Integration into a Professional Practices in Parasitology of Bioanalysis Course: Preliminary results

*Rowland Saer Hurtado, Salvador Bucella, and Yasmin Tang*

*University of Carabobo*

Laboratory Professional Practices in Parasitology is taught for final year bioanalysis students in the health sciences program at the University of Carabobo, Venezuela. We use Tablet PCs and digital ink in the laboratory classroom to support our teaching and learning environment. The pen-based technologies are also used to teach elementary school children about intestinal parasitic disease prevention. The professor's explanations, using pen-based technology in combination with Classroom Presenter software, enhances teacher-student interaction at both individual and group levels by providing immediate access to images and providing a collaborative learning environment. The approach also contributes to more accurate identification of the parasites found in specimens examined from different microscopes in the laboratory.

Our project has begun to yield preliminary results. We administered four different surveys to our students. In one of these, related to the use of pen-based technology, we have processed data from 68 student surveys administered in 2009 (61.8 percent of 110 student participants) and from 85 surveys in 2010 (68 percent of 125 student participants). These surveys included questions about student satisfaction, previous experience with the use of Tablet PCs, perceived usefulness of the Tablet PCs and the pen-based tools, as well as many other questions. The survey results show a trend toward student satisfaction with the use of these types of technology tools and suggest that these tools can be powerful for teaching health education to children.

# Effective Decision Making
# in the Age of Cloud Computing

*Gino Sorcinelli*

*University of Massachusetts Amherst*

"Effective Decision Making in the Age of Cloud Computing" is a university-based, multicultural seminar where students at the University of Massachusetts Amherst, the National University of Ireland Galway, and the National University of Ireland Maynooth use Tablet PCs and cloud software to achieve the following high-impact learning outcomes: a) collaborating with students locally and overseas; b) distilling information into manageable categories; c) mastering problem-solving skills; and d) presenting and publishing completed work. These are the skills students need to make effective decisions.

In class, students use Tablet PCs and the teleconferencing capabilities of ConferenceXP (CXP) to form multicultural teams and begin course-related on-line research assignments. During the semester, students use Tablet PC inking for note-taking on this research. Students access digital databases in the libraries on each campus to complete their research. At regular intervals during the semester, student teams teleconference using CXP on their Tablet PCs to update other teams on their research findings.

During the semester, students use Tablet PCs to save content (delivered by PowerPoint 2010) in OneNote 2010 workbooks. These OneNote files are saved to SharePoint 2010. The SharePoint server functions as the cloud presence for the class, making these files accessible by students via smart phones or other intelligent devices.

On a regular basis during the semester, students use their Tablet PCs for filling out course evaluation instruments such as pre-, mid-, and post-term questionnaires about course content, team-based learning, and how the knowledge they learned will be applied when they graduate.

# Index